Horizon

AUTUMN, 1971 · VOLUME XIII, NUMBER 4

Horizon

AUTUMN, 1971 · VOLUME XIII, NUMBER 4

EDITOR IN CHIEF
Joseph J. Thorndike

EDITOR
Charles L. Mee, Jr.
MANAGING EDITOR: Robert Cowley
ART EDITOR: Jane Wilson
ART DIRECTOR: Kenneth Munowitz
ASSOCIATE EDITORS: Shirley Tomkievicz, Ormonde de Kay, Jr.
CONTRIBUTING EDITORS: Walter Karp, Barbara Klaw
ASSISTANT EDITOR: Mary Sherman Parsons
EDITORIAL ASSISTANTS: W. Jeffrey Simpson, Susan Ferris
COPY EDITOR: Mary Ann Pfeiffer
ASSISTANT COPY EDITOR: Kaethe Ellis
ASSISTANT TO THE EDITOR: J. Muriel Vrotsos
ROVING EDITOR: Frederic V. Grunfeld

ADVISORY BOARD
Gilbert Highet, *Chairman,* Frederick Burkhardt,
William Harlan Hale, John Walker
EUROPEAN CONSULTING EDITOR: J. H. Plumb, *Christ's College, Cambridge*
CHIEF, EUROPEAN BUREAU: Gertrudis Feliu, *11 rue du Bouloi, Paris 1er*

AMERICAN HERITAGE PUBLISHING COMPANY
PRESIDENT AND PUBLISHER
Paul Gottlieb
EDITORIAL ART DIRECTOR
Murray Belsky
SENIOR EDITORS, HORIZON
Marshall B. Davidson
Oliver Jensen

HORIZON is published every three months by American Heritage Publishing Co., Inc. Editorial and executive offices: 551 Fifth Avenue, New York, N.Y. 10017. Treasurer: Marjorie C. Dyer. Secretary: John C. Taylor 3rd. All correspondence about subscriptions should be addressed to: HORIZON Subscription Office, 379 West Center St., Marion, Ohio 43302.

Single copies: $6.00. Subscriptions: $20.00 per year in the U.S. and Canada; elsewhere, $21.00.

Cumulative indexes for Volumes I–V and VI–X are available at $3. HORIZON is also indexed in the *Readers' Guide to Periodical Literature.* The editors welcome contributions but can assume no responsibility for unsolicited material. Title registered U.S. Patent Office. Second-class postage paid at New York, N.Y., and at additional mailing offices.

At the Bar of Bentham

In his model jail Jeremy Bentham weighs further "felicific" reforms.

According to Jeremy Bentham, the cranky British sage whose story is told by J. W. Burrow beginning on page 42, all the things of this world should be cross-examined like defendants at a trial. The chief question each must answer is: how much use do we, the members of the human race, get out of them? In Bentham's view, any human activity, custom, law, or institution could be measured by the amount of pleasure it provided multiplied by the number of people it pleased minus the quantity of pain it caused. By means of this "Felicific Calculus," as Bentham called his method, the philosopher of utility sought to bring all human things before the bar of usefulness, to be found guilty or not guilty. The jury, of course, was to be made up of Benthamites.

As Mr. Burrow relates, a great number of people found the Benthamite philosophy obnoxious, and Bentham's influential disciples more obnoxious still. Critics from Coleridge to Dickens pointed out that the depths and quirks of human life, the myriad bits and pieces that contribute to human felicity, simply could not be measured, either by the clumsy scale of the Felicific Calculus or by the criterion of utility in general. Their argument is, we think, amply confirmed by a quick perusal, with Bentham in mind, of this issue of HORIZON.

On page 56, for example, Bernard Rudofsky begins his fascinating account of the "fashionable body" through the ages. His theme—developed with a certain Benthamite bite—is the universal determination of mankind to pinch, cinch, stretch, scar, and otherwise mortify its flesh to meet some standard of bodily beauty to which the human frame seldom conforms. How would the Felicific Calculus deal with that mixture of pain and pleasure that so many people feel when they appear in public in some suitable approximation of the current mode? Clearly, it is difficult to strike a balance between the aesthetic pleasure of showing off one's stylishly pointed shoes and the pain of pinched toes.

On the other hand, Benthamites need have no compunctions about reading Frederic V. Grunfeld's account of the life of Mozart, which starts on page 96. Bentham himself both loved and felicifically approved of music; consequently, Mozart, on the Benthamite scale, must surely have met the highest standard of utility.

In his essay on Bentham, Mr. Burrow points out that human spontaneity—the sheer joy in *not* making Benthamite calculations—formed no part of the Benthamite philosophy. This side of human nature shows its relative benignity in Bruce Mazlish's essay on the ascetic revolutionaries, beginning on page 48. According to Professor Mazlish, there will be no revolutionary upheaval in America as long as the nation's rebellious youth continues to enjoy certain non-Benthamite pleasures. As Professor Mazlish makes clear, the serious revolutionary, from Robespierre to Mao Tse-tung, has been cut from a very different—indeed, a rather Benthamite—cloth.

Lastly, we might look at the Edwardian age, which J. H. Plumb vividly portrays, with all its dark inequities and all its glittering and apparently useless highlights. How do we make a felicific calculation about this contradictory epoch? A verdict would be difficult to reach, for as Dr. Plumb concludes, it is only the highlights of the Edwardian age that remain fixed in our memories. And how is one to weigh and measure, among the slippery bits and pieces that go to make up human felicity, the refreshing memory of ebullient times and radiant people?

What all this proves, perhaps, is that nothing final can be said about the constituents of human happiness. No man or group can ever devise a comprehensive scheme for producing, in Bentham's phrase, "the greatest happiness for the greatest number." The constituents of human happiness are far too varied and subtle for that, which is exactly why America's founders promised not happiness but the freedom to pursue it according to our own wisdom and folly, Benthamite or otherwise. —W.K.

COVER: A fisherman recently found this life-size mask of an Olmec ruler embedded beneath the bank of a river in the Mexican state of Veracruz. It adds to the rapidly growing stock of knowledge about this enigmatic culture, the first of the great Indian civilizations of America. The incisions on the mask, which is more than twenty-five centuries old, represent various Olmec gods. An article on the Olmecs by Michael D. Coe begins on page 66.
EDWARD H. MERRIN GALLERY, NEW YORK—JUSTIN KERR

Bruce Nauman's "Portrait of the Artist as a Fountain," 1966.

"Non-art," "anti-art," "non-art art," and "anti-art art" are useless.

If someone says his work is art, it's art.*

A non-art article on art

By THOMAS MEEHAN

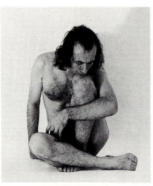

Vito Acconci's "Trademarks": the artist bites his naked body.

"Self-Burial" by Keith Arnatt: the artist explains, *"The content of my work is the strategy employed to ensure that there is no content other than the strategy."*

"All right," said the cat, and this time it vanished quite slowly, beginning with the end of the tail, and ending with the grin, which remained some time after the rest of it had gone.

"Well! I've often seen a cat without a grin," thought Alice, "but a grin without a cat! It's the most curious thing I ever saw in all my life!" —LEWIS CARROLL

Not long ago, Robert Barry, a thirty-five-year-old New York artist, was thinking about creating a work of art, though he hadn't the slightest idea of what it would be. In the bewildering world of contemporary art, however, Barry's idea that he might soon have an idea was itself deemed to be a work of art, and his singularly abstract creation was placed on exhibit at the Institute of Contemporary Art in London. That is, the institute displayed a typewritten card from the artist saying that he was on the intellectual track of "something which is very near in place and time, but not yet known to me." And as far as Barry himself was concerned, the act of having typed and mailed off the card closed the matter, for he'd thus done all that he felt was expected of him as an artist—a way of creating art that is certainly a good deal easier than, say, lying on your back for four years to paint the ceiling of the Sistine Chapel.

Barry, who, depending on one's view of such work, has either reduced art to its purest form or its most idiotic, is one of the better-known creators of a new and exceedingly cerebral style that is known as Conceptual Art—an all-inclusive term that might serve to de-

"Holograms": Nauman "making faces"

scribe the diverse activities of several hundred young American and foreign artists who, besides working with ideas, also deal with such tangible materials as earth, water, television sets, ice, mirrors, Xerox machines, *Roget's Thesaurus*, and their own kneecaps.

Involving himself with vague concepts of unknown concepts, Barry is inarguably at the outer limits of the form. Perhaps more typical of the Conceptual Artists is Vito Acconci, a thirty-one-year-old teacher at the School of Visual Arts in New York. Acconci, at any rate, has specific concepts rather than merely concepts of concepts. Last year, for example, when the Museum of Modern Art in New York put on a show of Conceptual Art that it called "Information," Acconci's entry was a work entitled "Service Area," which was exactly this: during the run of the show, that is, from July 2 until Septem-

ber 20, 1970, Acconci had his mail forwarded to himself at the museum. So, along with a typewritten sheet describing his concept, visitors to the show saw Acconci's telephone bill, appeals from the United Fund, and other pieces of mail stacked on a corner table.

His own contribution—or performance, as he termed it—was to drop around to the museum every few days to pick up his mail. "My performing here means reacting to stimuli (wanting or needing mail, fearing that mail might be stolen)," wrote Acconci in the catalogue for the show. "Performing the piece means going against form (the materials decrease as I pick up the mail). If I do not perform, the materials build up (the mail increases) while I am at rest. Left alone, the mail seeks equilibrium, which would be reached at the end of the exhibition (all the mail together in one place: saturation)." The ostensible point of "Service Area," like the point of much of Conceptual Art, was to cause the museum goer to look upon something perfectly ordinary—in this case, the process of receiving mail—with heightened perception.

"Service Area" is an example of a work of Conceptual Art that was not only thought up but also realized, i.e., Acconci actually had his mail forwarded to the museum. Frequently, however, the Conceptual Artist is satisfied simply to have the idea for a work and to leave it pretty much at that. Walter De Maria, a thirty-six-year-old California-born artist living in New York, had an idea a few years ago for a work called "Art Yard," which he described in part as follows:

Acconci's "Service Area": the artist goes to New York's Museum of Modern Art to pick up his mail from a table in—the service area.

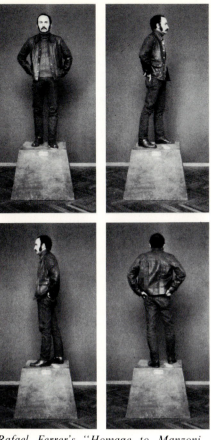

Rafael Ferrer's "Homage to Manzoni—Base Magica": the artist stands on a pedestal in a museum, thus becoming a work of art.

I have been thinking about an art yard I would like to build. It would be sort of a big hole in the ground. Actually it wouldn't be a hole to begin with. That would have to be dug. The digging of the hole would be part of the art. Luxurious stands would be made for the art lovers and spectators to sit in.

They would come to the making of the yard dressed in tuxedos and clothes which would make them aware of the significance of the event they would see. Then in front of the stand of people a wonderful parade of steamshovels and bulldozers will pass. Pretty soon the steamshovels would start to dig. And small explosions would go off. What wonderful art will be produced.

De Maria didn't literally expect to dig "Art Yard," and would probably have been surprised if anyone had taken him seriously about it. As another Conceptual Artist, Sol LeWitt, says, "The idea itself, even if not made visual, is as much a work of art as any finished product." Thus, there are two basic styles of Conceptual Art: the realized concept and the unrealized. Most Conceptual Artists work at one time or another in both styles, although there

is a growing feeling among them that the unrealized concept—the grin without the cat—is the purer form of the art.

If the Conceptual Artist doesn't necessarily have to realize his concepts, one perplexedly wonders, does he have to possess any particular talent for art in the traditional sense—like, say, the ability to draw a straight line? Answer: No. The need for training in such disciplines as drawing, painting, and sculpture is for the most part entirely irrelevant to Conceptual Art, though many of the artists have such training. In fact, a group of Conceptual Artists who call themselves Language Artists deal entirely with words rather than with visual objects or even with ideas for visual objects. Joseph Kosuth, for example, who is perhaps the best known of the American Language Artists, has turned out blown-up copies of dictionary definitions or excerpts from *Roget's Thesaurus,* the most famous of which is his copy of the definition of the word "definition." Kosuth has also taken out classified ads in mass-circulation newspapers and magazines, like the one he inserted recently in *The New York Times:* "1. Existence. A. Being in the Abstract. 1. Existence. 2. Nonexistence." "It is impossible to see my work," says Kosuth. "What is seen is the presentation of the information. The art exists only as an invisible, ethereal idea."

At the moment the art world is in a state of considerable excitement

Dennis Oppenheim's "Parallel Stress," 1970

Don Graham's "Roll": the artist rolls around photographing a camera photographing him photographing the camera photographing.

about Language Art, or Post-Object Art, as it is sometimes known, or "art as idea as idea," as Kosuth describes it; for a number of art critics feel that it represents a major step toward doing away entirely with the visual object in art, which many are beginning to suspect is the ultimate aim of modern art. On the other hand, the peripheral observer, like me, can't help but think that the Language Artists have stumbled on something that for thousands of years has been called writing.

Much of Conceptual Art is so irrational and difficult to understand, so seemingly downright crazy, that one is led immediately to wonder if the movement might not be a monumental put-on by a cabal of artists who are out to test the gullibility of the international art world to its utmost limits. De Maria fills each of three rooms in a Munich gallery with three feet of dirt; Iain Baxter urinates in a field inside the Arctic Circle; Rafael Ferrer drags hundreds of pounds of ice onto the entrance ramp of the

7

Les Levine's "Paint," says the gallery press release, "is a show of wet paint." The photograph here is "information concerning the act of pouring out the paint."

Whitney Museum to let it melt—and all these activities are called works of art.

Surely, Conceptual Art is a joke, and yet this is what the Philistine has said at the outset of every modernist art movement. And years later, as in the case of those who thought that Marcel Duchamp's *Nude Descending a Staircase* was a joke when it was first exhibited at the 1913 Armory Show, the Philistine must eat his words. Yesterday's incomprehensible work of the avant-garde, like Duchamp's painting, is today's framed reproduction over the fireplace in a Grosse Point living room. And no matter how absurd much of their work may seem, the Conceptual Artists, for better or worse, aren't kidding. In fact, they're dedicated, intelligent, and exceedingly serious young men, even if they themselves admit there is an element of playfulness and the put-on to some of Conceptual Art.

If they're serious, however, what exactly is it that they're serious about? In the first place, the Conceptual Artist firmly believes that the traditional forms of art, like paintings and works of sculpture, have reached a dead end. And, moreover, that they're anachronistically irrelevant in an age of computers, space travel, xerography, and such forms of instant visual communication as picture telephones and color television sets. Secondly, the Conceptual Artist believes that art has for too long been boxed into museums and reverently worshiped, as though paintings and works of sculpture were the holy objects of some oppressive and humorless religion. A religion, too, in which the artist has been exploited, not only by museum directors, gallery owners, art collectors, and art critics, but also by those who merely file through museums to gaze with hushed awe at the works upon the wall.

The art world, as it presently exists, says the Conceptual Artist, must be totally destroyed, and it is this thinking that has led him to create works that, because of their ephemeral nature, can't be hung in museums or purchased by collectors. In short, the purest Conceptual Artist, who angrily wishes no longer to see reputations and fortunes made by others from the work of artists, is the anarchist of the art world, who wouldn't be unhappy to see every museum in the world blown up.

Paradoxically, a number of museums and galleries both here and in Europe, including in New York the Museum of Modern Art, the Whitney Museum, the Jewish Museum, the New York Cultural Center, and the Dwan and Leo Castelli galleries, have in the past several years mounted shows of Conceptual Art. What is seen at such shows, however, is more often the so-called documentation of a work of Conceptual Art rather than the work itself. Dennis Oppenheim, for instance, a thirty-three-year-old California artist who lives today in New York, created a work last year called "Hay Maze," which was exhibited at a Manhattan gallery in the form of photographs of a realized concept. To create "Hay Maze," Oppenheim journeyed to White-

8

water, Wisconsin, where he persuaded a farmer to lend him an alfalfa field, 1,200 bales of hay, and a couple of wagonloads of corn. Then, with the help of twenty-five art students from Wisconsin State University, which is located in Whitewater, he placed the bales of hay around the field in such a way as to form a geometric maze, dumped the corn in the center of the maze, and drove a herd of Holsteins through the maze to the corn. Thus, "Hay Maze," an ephemeral work of Conceptual Art that ceased to exist the moment the Holsteins reached the corn.

A further paradox: Conceptual Art has been latched on to by private collectors of art. Robert C. Scull, the famed New York collector of Pop Art, has commissioned much of the recent work of Michael Heizer, a twenty-seven-year-old California-born artist who involves himself mainly in the area of Conceptual Art that is known as Earth Art (or, as certain negative critics have disgustedly termed it, Boulderdash). In his early work Heizer dug trenches in the ground, like the foot-deep, 120-foot-long trench that he did in the shape of a circumflex a while ago at Massacre Dry Lake, near Vya, Nevada. The work, starkly entitled "Circumflex," was one of nine similar efforts that had been commissioned by Scull, who in return for his money got photographs of the trench for his art

collection—in other words, documentation of the work.

Heizer, by the way, describes his trenches as "negative objects." The art world, he feels, is already impossibly full of objects, so he refuses to make any more. "Artists have been misled into thinking that you have to create something in order to contribute to art," says Heizer. "I want to create without creating a thing." He explains, moreover, that "in the desert, I can find that kind of unraped, peaceful, religious space artists have always tried to put into their work. I don't want any indication I've been here at all. My holes should have no history, they should be indeterminate in time and inaccessible in locale." When Heizer had finished "Circumflex," which took him about a day to dig, he met Scull in Las Vegas, and the two then went out to the remote site of the work. "I have nothing left but the memory of a superb experience and a precise documentation of all that Heizer did," Scull later remarked. "Art is only memory anyway," said Heizer.

Besides Scull, other well-known private collectors of Conceptual Art include Ray Kaufman, a New York businessman; Horace Solomon, a New York manufacturing executive; John de Menil, a Houston oil millionaire; and a number of Europeans, such as

Ferrer's "Ice": melting into autumn leaves on the ramp of New York's Whitney Museum.

Pepino Agrati, a Milan industrialist. Still, most Conceptual Art doesn't get bought by anybody, and the typical Conceptual Artist must support himself by some such job as teaching. In short, he's usually as poor in a financial way as his art is poor in objective substance. (The Italians refer to Conceptual Art as art *povera*, or impoverished art.) On the other hand, the documentation of most works of Conceptual Art is generally for sale. And dealers have gotten into the act, too. Among them is John Gibson, a thirty-eight-year-old New York artists' representative, who deals almost exclusively in the sale of Conceptual Art documentation and is the representative or agent for ten of the leading Conceptual Artists, including Acconci, Oppenheim, Dan Graham, and Christo Javacheff.

Gibson has lately been staging so-called performances of Conceptual Art for student audiences in New York and its environs. Not long ago, he produced an evening of the works of Dan Graham for a couple of hundred students at New York University, each of whom paid two dollars to attend the performance. The evening was made up of ten works of Conceptual Art done on the spot by Graham, typical of which was "Lax/Relax." Before the performance a girl named Charlotte Townsend had repeated the word "relax" into a tape recorder for fifteen

Walter De Maria dumped "Pure Dirt, Pure Earth, Pure Land" into a Munich gallery in 1968.

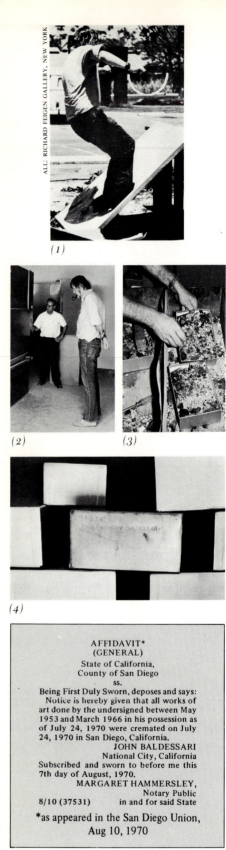

(1)

(2)   *(3)*

(4)

AFFIDAVIT*
(GENERAL)
State of California,
County of San Diego
ss.
Being First Duly Sworn, deposes and says:
Notice is hereby given that all works of
art done by the undersigned between May
1953 and March 1966 in his possession as
of July 24, 1970 were cremated on July
24, 1970 in San Diego, California.
JOHN BALDESSARI
National City, California
Subscribed and sworn to before me this
7th day of August, 1970.
MARGARET HAMMERSLEY,
Notary Public
8/10 (37531)   in and for said State

*as appeared in the San Diego Union,
Aug 10, 1970

(5)

John Baldessari's "Cremation Piece": the artist (1) smashed his paintings, (2) had them burned in a California crematorium, (3) put the ashes in boxes, and (4) had them buried in a wall of the Jewish Museum during its 1970 "Software" exhibition. A notary public "in and for" the State of California attested (5) to the realization of his concept.

minutes. Then, during the performance, the tape was played back while Graham stood before the audience chanting the word "lax." The audience, he later explained, became at once self-conscious and involved, which was supposedly the point of the work.

An increasing number of Conceptual Artists are working these days with various devices of modern technology —that is, turning out works that involve tape recorders, like "Lax/Relax," or that make use of such equipment as video-tape recorders, closed-circuit television systems, movie cameras, movie projectors, and computers. In a work called "TV Camera/Monitor Performance," for example, Graham rolled around on a table for several minutes, holding a television camera, while an image of this activity and the heads of the spectators was projected on a monitor at the rear of the audience. And Edwin Morgan uses computers to turn out "code poems," as he terms them. A typical one goes like this: "TEYZA PRQTP ZSNSX OSRMY VCFBO . . ." And so on for sixty-seven additional and equally incomprehensible words.

Vito Acconci has given up forwarding his mail and similar works to experiment with a new form of Conceptual Art known as Body Art. In Body Art, which at least one critic has called the most significant artistic breakthrough in several years, the principal material used to create the work is the artist's own body. "Variously called actions, events, performances, pieces, things, the works present physical activities, ordinary bodily functions and other usual and unusual manifestations of physicality," *Avalanche,* a quarterly journal of all categories of Conceptual Art, recently explained. "The artist's body becomes both the subject and the object of the work." Three examples of works by Acconci, however, might give a better idea of what Body Art is about:

Example 1: "Rubbing Piece." Sitting alone in a booth in a New York restaurant called Max's Kansas City, Acconci rubbed his left forearm with the fingers of his right hand until a sore was produced. To document the work, photographs were taken by a young lady named Betsy Jackson.

Example 2: "Hand and Mouth Piece." In his Christopher Street apartment, Acconci shoved his left hand into his mouth until he began to choke and was forced to remove it. He repeated this activity for six minutes. Documentation of the work exists in the form of a three-minute 8 mm. film in black and white and a six-minute 16 mm. film in color.

Example 3: "Trademarks." Sitting naked on the floor of his apartment, Acconci bit every part of his body that he could reach with his mouth. In each instance, he bit hard enough for teeth marks to show. Next, he applied printer's ink to the bites and used himself as a human stamp "to stamp bite-prints on various surfaces." This activity was also photographed.

The documentation of works such as "Rubbing Piece," "Hand and Mouth

PUBLISHED IN *Artforum*

Robert Morris advertises his services.

*A wholly imaginary gallery
for purely fictitious artists.*

Piece," and "Trademarks" can be purchased through John Gibson for approximately six hundred dollars apiece. Adds *Avalanche* on Body Art, "Aesthetic considerations aside, it is not surprising that under the present repressive socio-economic situation young artists have turned to their most readily available source, themselves, for sculptural material with almost unlimited potential, capable of doing exactly what the artist wants, without the obduracy of inanimate matter." Acconci, by the way, sometimes invites art critics to his apartment to witness his performances, but most of these critics don't feel that it is necessary to see him at work in order to understand what he is doing. "I report on Acconci without having seen him do his act," writes the distinguished art critic Harold Rosenberg. "Why should anyone see him? That his art is exactly like anything else is the point of it."

If there is an underlying philosophy to Conceptual Art, it is that everything in the world, from Acconci's left forearm to the Gobi Desert, is potentially art. Thus Robert Morris, a well-known and versatile artist, can have a crew of workmen haul tons of concrete blocks, twelve-foot timbers, and steel pipes up

to the third-floor gallery of the Whitney Museum, instruct them to dump everything more or less randomly on the floor, and label the result a work of sculpture entitled, with a certain poverty of imagination, "Untitled."

" 'Non-art,' 'anti-art,' 'non-art art,' and 'anti-art art' are useless. If someone says his work is art, it's art," says the Minimal and Conceptual Artist Donald Judd in what amounts virtually to a manifesto of the movement. Harold Rosenberg essentially agrees. As he has observed, even a painted plank can be considered a work of sculpture: "As a sculpture, a painted plank is not only its material substance but the crystallization of a moment in the continuous debate on the nature of art—an intellectual element missing from planks in lumberyards." In short, because an artist selects a specific painted plank to call a work of sculpture, the plank *is* a work of sculpture.

A group of Conceptual Artists who might be called Site Artists designate entire geographic areas, or sites, as works of art. Recently, for example, five areas of Franklin, New Jersey, were so designated by Robert Smithson. And, going even further, Smithson involves himself with non-sites: with maps, photographs, typewritten descriptions of places, and geologic samples.

Then, too, there are non-galleries, or at least there is one. Last winter Terry Fugate-Wilcox, a young artist from

Kalamazoo, Michigan, set up the Jean Freeman Gallery at 26 West 57th Street in New York and advertised shows of Conceptual Art in several major art magazines. The Jean Freeman Gallery did not exist, however, nor is there such a New York address as 26 West 57th Street. Fugate-Wilcox has since designated his "non-gallery of no art," as *The New York Times* called it, a work of Conceptual Art.

Looked on as an isolated phenomenon, Conceptual Art is extraordinarily difficult to make much sense out of. When viewed as a stage in the evolution of modern art in America since the 1913 Armory Show, however, it begins to make at least a little sense. Essentially, all of avant-garde art, from Duchamp's *Nude Descending a Staircase* to Acconci's "Trademarks," has been a movement toward total abstraction. For a while the work of some of the abstract expressionists, like Mark Rothko, Barnett Newman, and Clyfford Still, seemed to have carried this movement to its ultimate end. But then, a few years ago, along came Minimalists like the late Ad Reinhardt, who turned out a series of almost totally black canvases that have been described as "the material equivalents of the silences of his Trappist friend, Thomas Merton." Said Reinhardt, "I'm just making the last paintings that anyone can make." Thus, doing away with paintings and sculpture altogether,

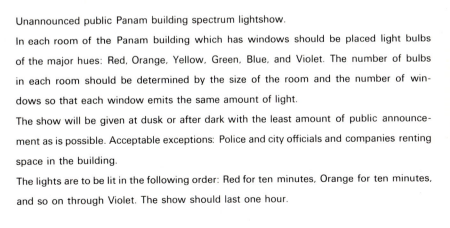

Unannounced public Panam building spectrum lightshow.

In each room of the Panam building which has windows should be placed light bulbs of the major hues: Red, Orange, Yellow, Green, Blue, and Violet. The number of bulbs in each room should be determined by the size of the room and the number of windows so that each window emits the same amount of light.

The show will be given at dusk or after dark with the least amount of public announcement as is possible. Acceptable exceptions: Police and city officials and companies renting space in the building.

The lights are to be lit in the following order: Red for ten minutes, Orange for ten minutes, and so on through Violet. The show should last one hour.

Stephen Kaltenbach's spectrum light show: never done, it still exists—in the minds of our readers.

Michael Heizer's "Double Negative": geologic time intersects with the history of art as the artist ascends one of the troughs bulldozed from the walls of a Nevada mesa. Heizer, who describes his trenches as "negative objects," feels that the art world is already too full of the positive kind.

and dealing simply with ideas about art—i.e., Conceptual Art—can be seen as the next logical step forward.

And Conceptual Art certainly owes a debt to the Dadaists, like Duchamp and Man Ray, who more than a half century ago proclaimed that such ordinary objects as a bicycle wheel, a wine rack, and a men's room urinal were works of art. By the logic, or illogic, of Dada, which is also the logic of Conceptual Art, anything that the artist calls art is art. In consequence, there's no necessity to turn out paintings or works of sculpture of any kind. Dada,

however, arising before painting and sculpture had at last "exhausted" themselves in Minimalism, was fifty years ahead of its time. And Conceptual Art in the form of the unrealized concept goes a step beyond Dada in that the artist wouldn't go to the trouble of literally sending a men's room urinal to a gallery—he'd simply propose that it be done and let it go at that. Within a couple of years, in fact, since fewer and fewer concepts are being realized, Conceptual Art will probably consist only of proposed ideas that are never to be realized. The ideal and ultimate medium of Conceptual Art, wrote Jack Burnham not long ago in *Artforum* magazine, is mental telepathy.

Perhaps the earliest known works of Conceptual Art were a series of unrealizable proposals that Duchamp made in a book entitled *Marchand du Sel,* which was published in 1958. About the same time, a group of European artists who called themselves the New Realists experimented with works of the absurd that critics now consider to have been Conceptual Art. A French artist named Yves Klein exhibited a work in Paris that he called "Empty Gallery," which was, as its title strongly suggests, nothing more than an empty gallery. In the United States during the

mid-sixties Joseph Kosuth began to work with ephemeral materials. In 1965 he created what has been spoken of as the first American work of Conceptual Art—a five-foot-square sheet of glass entitled "Any Five-Foot Sheet of Glass to Lean Against Any Wall."

The following year, 1966, a number of young American artists, including Sol LeWitt, Robert Morris, and Donald Judd, began to turn out works of Conceptual Art. At first, each realized his concepts, and it wasn't until the spring of 1968 that the concept of the unrealized concept was stumbled upon by Lawrence Weiner, a New York painter who was one of the earliest Site Artists. In May, 1968, while participating in an art symposium at Windham College in Putney, Vermont, Weiner laid out a site on campus that he outlined with stakes and lengths of string—the enclosed site, he said, was a work of Site Art. Nonsense, said an outraged group of Windham students, who proceeded angrily to cut his string, and it was at that moment that Weiner understood he needn't have bothered to put out the stakes and string, "for the effect of the piece had already been made in suggesting it." Back in New York, Weiner discussed his revelation with a number of his artist friends, including Robert Barry, Douglas Huebler, and Kosuth, and thus did the concept of the unrealized concept swiftly spread to the American art world.

The earliest of the Conceptual Artists to get wide public attention were the Earth Artists, including Michael Heizer, Robert Morris, Dennis Oppenheim, and Walter De Maria, who in October, 1968, exhibited mainly photographic documentation of their works in a group show called "Earthworks." "Earthworks," perhaps the most talked about and publicized art show of the 1968 fall season, was made up of such works as photographs of trenches, mounds of rock and dirt, a grave-sized hole, and a model of the patterns cut in Kansas wheat fields. "Earthworks" was actually the first major American show of Conceptual

"Threaded Calabash Project" by Peter Hutchinson: gourds are tied to a Tobago reef.

Robert Smithson's "Spiral Jetty": a fifteen-hundred-foot spiral of landfill was built out into Great Salt Lake in Utah.

Art, although the form was then generally termed Impossible Art, for the reason that it was impossible to bring it into a gallery or to buy and sell it.

"Earthworks" led in the next year and a half to a number of other shows of Earth Art, both in the United States and abroad. Earth Art, however, or Ecological Art, as it is now more fashionably termed, is today somewhat passé, and many of the Earth Artists have abandoned earth to work with other materials. Heizer is still at it, though, and was reported recently to be trying to find a mountaintop out West where he can "displace" a large mass of rock and put it firmly into a nearby hole. Heizer plans to do this by old-fashioned block-and-tackle techniques and hopes his site will be high enough so that "anybody who wants to see it will have to risk his life."

From earth a number of Conceptual Artists, including Peter Hutchinson, a young Englishman who now lives in New York, went on to water—specifically, they turned out works of un-

derwater sculpture, like Hutchinson's "Threaded Calabash Project," which, as a photograph documents, is five calabash fruits strung together on a rope that is anchored to a coral reef under thirty feet of water off Tobago in the West Indies. Meanwhile, other Conceptual Arts turned to Skyworks, that is, they shot beams of light of varying intensity into the night sky, and to Burial Works, which involved such activities as burying a steel cube in a garden in Holland, as Sol LeWitt did sev-

Smithson's "Mirror Displacement": the statement is the reflection, partially buried in Yucatán—as Eliot might have said, "A heap of broken images, where the sun beats . . ."

eral years ago. And finally, led by Robert Barry, Barry La Va, and Lawrence Weiner, the Conceptual Artists have lately been abandoning materials altogether to turn out proposals for projects that aren't intended to be realized. Which is the point of progress, or nonprogress, at which Conceptual Art currently stands.

Among the more intriguing recent proposals for an unrealizable concept is "Cement Store," a work by a California Pop sculptor named Edward Kienholz, who occasionally turns to Conceptual Art. For "Cement Store," Kienholz proposes that a hole be drilled in the roof of a "grocery store in a town anywhere in the United States with a population of less than 5,000" and cement poured in until the store is filled up to the ceiling with the stuff. And Claes Oldenburg, the Pop Artist who is also into Conceptual Art today, has proposed (1) that a giant banana be erected in the middle of Times Square in New York; and (2) that an enormous toilet-tank float be anchored in the

13

river Thames in such a way that it would rise and fall with the tides. Oldenburg calls it "Thames Ball," but "London, W.C. 1" might do just as well.

Because most of their concepts aren't intended to be realized, many of the Conceptual Artists tend to think on a rather grand scale, like putting a towering model of a Good Humor Bar on Park Avenue in New York, as Oldenburg has also proposed. None of them thinks on a grander scale than does Christo Javacheff, a thirty-six-year-old Bulgarian-born artist now living in New York, and Javacheff, or Christo, as he is usually known, realizes most of his concepts, too. Christo, whose works of Conceptual Art are unique, is obsessed with wrapping familiar objects in such materials as paper, canvas, and plastic in order to "disrupt the viewer's normal relationship with ordinary elements and excite his curiosity through veiling their forms." He began in 1958 by wrapping relatively small objects, like Coca-Cola bottles, easy chairs, and naked girls; but a penchant for gigantism later overtook him, and by February, 1969, he had wrapped the entire Museum of Contemporary Art in Chicago in ten thousand square feet of canvas and four thousand feet of Manila rope. And in November, 1969, he wrapped a mile of the Australian seacoast in one million square feet of plastic and thirty-five miles of rope.

"Packaging—meaning to contain an object by itself in a most realistic way —exposes its commonness in a beautiful and relaxed manner," says Christo. To accomplish his larger works, Christo uses squads of assistants, and his giant packages cost tens of thousands of dollars to realize. "Wrapped Coast," for instance, as he called his Australian work, took a crew of sixty volunteers more than a month to install, was underwritten by private individuals, and took place on a stretch of coast owned by a Sydney hospital. The hospital, in

Christo's "Valley Curtain": this summer it spanned Rifle Gap in Colorado, but the passage of wildlife, the migratory movement of the birds, and the natural ecology of the area were not disrupted.

fact, eventually made money on the project by charging twenty cents apiece to the curious who came out from Sydney to gaze upon the work. Christo was unhappy when the directors of the hospital ordered him to unwrap the coast after it had been under plastic for only four weeks, but he took his unhappiness philosophically. "It's not a very permanent world, anyway," he said with a shrug of his shoulders.

Christo is also responsible for perhaps the most spectacular work of art done in the United States this year— "Valley Curtain," a 250,000-square-foot rectangle of orange nylon that was hung on a 1,375-foot-long steel cable this summer between a pair of rocky peaks 250 and 400 feet high in the mountains of central Colorado near Aspen. "Valley Curtain," something of a departure from Christo's usual packaging, was put up last June by a crew of engineers and construction men, hung during July and August in such a way as to curtain off an entire Colorado valley, and is now in the process of being taken down. The work cost $200,-000, most of which was put up by European museums and collectors, which in return for their money will get documentation of the work. Why did Christo put up the curtain? "Because it was for me an exciting life experience—I don't care what anyone else thinks of it." Christo next hopes to wrap several of New York's larger skyscrapers in polypropylene plastic, although he sadly admits that this is in the nature of a proposal that will probably never be realized.

While many leading art critics, including Harold Rosenberg, Barbara Rose, and Jack Burnham, are cautiously enthusiastic about Conceptual Art, others deplore it. Hilton Kramer of *The New York Times* can't stand it. Conceptual Art, he writes, "is the latest species of esthetic escapism—in this case, an escape from mind itself. It would be lamentable even if it were not so egregiously boring, but in the end it is the sheer weight of its boredom that is most repellent."

Where can modern art conceivably progress to from Conceptual Art? One is strongly tempted to say nowhere, to announce that Conceptual Art is unequivocally the end of the line for modern art. On the other hand, that's exactly what some people said in the past about such movements as abstract expressionism and Minimalism. So, in the last analysis, who knows? Certainly not John Gibson, who when asked recently to speculate on where Conceptual Art was going and what might come after it, could only quote Mort Sahl's line, "The future lies ahead." A hint of the future may be contained, however, in a work of Conceptual Art by a young British artist named Keith Arnatt. The work is a series of photographs of Arnatt that show him sinking slowly downward into what appears to be quicksand until he has entirely vanished. And with him, in a symbolic sense, one can't help but feel that all of art as we have previously known it has also vanished. Still, if all else has vanished, Conceptual Art is with us, and one might conclude with a statement made by the artist Les Levine about one of his own works of Conceptual Art—"So what if it's stupid, at least it's something."

When not submitting concepts of concepts by postcard and video tape, Thomas Meehan is under wraps in Connecticut.

"Wrapped Coast": Christo covered a mile of Australian seashore with one million square feet of polypropylene plastic.

The Thurber Carnival

Looking back, I can see now that any one of a dozen books would have done the trick as nicely—just as any one of a dozen girls would have done for the Perfect Affair (if you hadn't met Maud first). But *The Thurber Carnival* had the great virtue of being there: a routine case of "the time and the place and the loved one together."

I can't even remember our first meeting—probably in the back of some little bookstore, the two of us surrounded by dust beams and old men reading with umbrellas between their knees. But I remember my predicament very well indeed. I was looking desperately for an antidote to England, particularly to the sound of England.

As a surly fifteen-year-old British war refugee press-ganged home from America, and into a posh school, in 1946, I had borne bravely enough with the appearance of the place—the basic Evelyn Waugh face, which rattled me some, and the ladies dressed in slip-covers—and even with the smell of tortured cabbage. But I was completely unstrung by the little boys who spoke like butlers, by the three-day-old corpse at the BBC who kept saying, "His Majesty's Government view with the *gravest* concern," and by the way this spooky language rolled out on the printed page.

It isn't every American voice that would have helped. I had already heard the tourists in the Tower of London, rumbling and shrilling and howling for Junior to come get a load of the antiquiddies. The ears of the homesick pass through tender phases in which just about everything prickles. After the tourists had gone, some English wise guy might pipe, "Hey, Mac, how old is this joint anyway?" and I would blush for both of them.

House and Woman

For anyone in this jumpy condition I can think of no writer more soothing than Thurber. To begin with, he was a near-blind raconteur, like Homer, so that his prose "sounds"; he had played it through on his own ear first. His voice was flat, after the English bird song, but not *too* flat. Where the English carried modulation to the brink of hysteria, his ups and downs were measured, and a delicate low music came of them. Later, I was to hear many English voices besides Southern Regional Fruity, and I realized that they could make a jolly decent noise; but by then, I had my book.

Maybe the reason I harp on voice so much is that I was not particularly taken by Thurber's subject matter at first. His sparring couples and quaint relatives seemed like the stock material of the baggy-pants writers, and his passion for dogs was beyond me. (Reading about dogs is almost as bad as having them stand on your chest and lick you.) In general, comic essayists tend to work with the same worn deck of cards, getting their effects with small variations of patter and style.

In Thurber's case there was a further complication: it turned out that the English liked him. To idolatry. (An old friend of his claims that this was finally

his undoing. Like S. J. Perelman, he wound up wanting to be an English gentleman. So much for my antidote.) Thus it became my mission to find out what the locals liked about him, and to like something different.

Well, of course, it was his delicious sense of humor that they, as it were, "dug," so I flung myself to the far extreme and maintained that he wasn't a humorist at all. A mistake, but a useful one, because it got both him and his fan out of a shallow, middle-brow category and into something like art. The Thurber relatives ceased to be comic-cut figures and became folk characters, the sparring couples were lost Americans—uprooted versions of Sherwood Anderson's midwesterners, defiant, eccentric, profoundly baffled. I never quite got to the Dog as Symbol —that one eludes me to this day.

It is much too late for me to tell whether this wealth of meaning is really in the book, or whether I made it all up. It's there for me. When Thurber himself tried to take his Ohio background seriously, in *The Thurber Album,* it went flat on him. He *was* a humorist—my Anglophobia finally cooled enough for me to admit that— and though *I* could think of him as a serious artist as well, it wasn't safe for *him* to do so. Anyway, he put me onto a new line of inquiry: Thurber, Ring Lardner, Anderson, Hemingway—to me this still looks like a straight line, even though I've got them in slightly the wrong order. The English (bah! what did they know?) took him for a cool *New Yorker* wit. I alone saw the wandering midwesterner, hot and restless inside his understated prose, who if anything romanticized *The New Yorker,* the way Gatsby romanticized East Egg, or Hemingway Pamplona.

By WILFRID SHEED

The other thing the English liked was the cartoons, and I had to give ground grudgingly on that, while reiterating, as he did himself, that he was primarily a writer. The only thing to do was to find the drawings that they didn't like and carry on about those. But here the wily natives had me: they liked all the right ones. "What Have You Done with Dr. Millmoss?" "I Said the Hounds of Spring Are on Winter's Traces—But Let it Pass, Let it Pass!" "That's My First Wife Up There, and This Is the *Present* Mrs. Harris."

This chased me into "The Pet Department"—but the British were right about that, too. "We have cats the way most people have mice." Smashing. "What you have is a bear." Super. I surrendered definitively over *Fables for Our Time*. The limeys liked "The Owl Who Was God" just as much as I did. And I began to see that they might have pretty good taste at that.

So this was another small service the book rendered: to reconcile me with my own people. The English are, in fact, the world's best, and noisiest, humor fans—the only trouble being that *everything* sets them off. Like Saint Paul, they approve the best but enjoy a giggle over the worst as well.

Rereading the book, I find that in my zeal to upstage my hosts, I had slightly overrated the straight serious pieces, like "One is a Wanderer" and "The Evening's at Seven," but that *they* had overrated the straight funny ones, like "The Night the Bed Fell."

Thurber's humorous style was not as unique as I had supposed it to be, but a brilliant fusion of several styles. The midwestern tall-story style was there, inherited from Mark Twain (whom Thurber claimed hardly to have read; but beware of what writers claim not to have read), speeded up slightly for

We have cats the way most people have mice.

"That's My First Wife Up There, and This Is the *Present* Mrs. Harris"

vaudeville slapstick effects and at the same time quieted down for the soft-spoken *New Yorker* house style. The Benchley-absurd and the Dorothy Parker-laconic were in there, too (e.g., a piece of pure Parker: "I left the newspaper game and drifted into the magazine game. And now, in closing, I wish to leave with my little readers, both boys and girls, this parting bit of advice: Stay out of the magazine game.") Thurber was a compulsive mimic, with a Venus's-flytrap of a memory. So in discovering him, I was also discovering American humor, and didn't know it.

But the pieces that hold up best are the ones in between. "The little wheels of [our] invention are set in motion by the damp hand of melancholy," he said; and when they actually were—and not just by the damp hand of editors—he was incomparable. Much nonsense has been talked about melancholy comedians, but there is no real melancholy in Benchley, Leacock, or W. S. Gilbert. Gruffness, maybe, as wit becomes a grunting middle-aged effort; grouchiness, as reality refuses to turn into something funny, even when you clobber it with your wand. But the tragedy of the aging clown is that he *cannot* feel melancholy.

Thurber was grouchy himself by the end, after some eighteen eye operations had left him as blind as none would have. He was, for all his disclaimers, a visual artist, he needed to see. But before that, he had achieved melancholy, fair and square. Stories like "The Breaking Up of the Winships" (where a light argument about the merits of Garbo vs. Donald Duck ends up destroying a marriage) or "The Curb in the Sky" (where the final scene has the wife correcting her husband's dreams in a mental home) have a strangled

horror about them that is outside the scope of the funnymen. His two best stories, for my money, "The Cane in the Corridor" and "Something to Say," combine a comic phrasing with a panic and darkness of heart to produce a third emotion: a kind of nerve-racked exhilaration, a mood you've never precisely had before, the test of Art. Thurber's own favorite author was Henry James, and the master's spirit is there in the quiet, doom-laden rooms, the desperate skirmishings of men and women. Now don't tell me this is a mere humorist.

To go out by the door we came in by: as my personal Voice of America, Thurber did mislead me slightly in one respect, through no fault of his own. Along with the rest of my homesick pantheon—George Gershwin, the Marx Brothers, and Fred Astaire—he hinted of an urban wonderland, a Manhattan of penthouses and town cars and excruciating wit, where bright boys and girls from all over lit up the night sky with wisecracks. When I fought my way back to America a year later (whined, wheedled, and threatened my parents with blackmail might describe it better), I found the place had vanished, if it ever had existed, and found myself so transatlantically tongue-tied that I couldn't have said "boo" to an Algonquin Wit if one had been delivered bound and gagged to our subleased apartment in the Bronx.

Wilfrid Sheed, the author of Office Politics *and* Max Jamison, *is now in Dublin, where his reputation as one of our best young novelists will doubtless pursue him.*

"What Have You Done with Dr. Millmoss?"

Edward VII and Queen Alexandra at the Cowes Regatta, 1909.

The Edwardians

The life-span of their age was brief, and they—the grandfathers and great-grandfathers of our own chaotic age—dashed stylishly from Victoria's funeral to World War I, not pausing to count the calories or the cost

By J. H. PLUMB

The annual regatta at Cowes on the Isle of Wight

She was dead at last. The German emperor had rushed across Europe to be at her deathbed; the Prince of Wales, an aging and corpulent *bon viveur*, had broken down and wept as she put out her feeble arms and called "Bertie." Her nation stood silent and stunned, waiting for the last moments to ebb away, and then broke into an orgy of lamentations. Three thousand poems bewailed the passing of Queen Victoria; newspapers in Calcutta, Rangoon,

was the glory of the Edwardian summer for American as well as British socialites. In 1909 the Vanderbilts dazzled Cowes with this party aboard their yacht.

Cape Town, and Montreal, in cities and countries throughout the world, printed elegies with borders as black and as deep as night. The Reverend R. C. Fillingham, widely known as the Radical Vicar of Hexton, wrote:

It is no time for speaking. Voice, be dumb!
The darkest day of England's years has come.
From peer's and peasants' eyes the tear-drops start
Each heart in England is a broken heart.

But dumb the English poets would not be. Even *The Agnostic Journal* burst into song, proclaiming for the queen, if not a heavenly, at least a historical immortality. The peerage had its poet in Lord Burghclere; the House of Commons, not to be outshone, produced an ode by William Allan, M.P.; Ella Wheeler Wilcox rhymed for America; Thomas Hardy produced one of his more unreadable lyrics; and there was "a very creditable effort . . . penned by

a working man," Mr. Egby of Reading.

The refrain, no matter how complex the variation of imagery and prosody, was often the same: the Great Mother of Empire had gone at last. In poem after poem there was a note of doom, a sense that the world would never be quite the same again. Mostly the poets looked back with nostalgia to Victoria's long reign. Those few who cast a thoughtful eye on the future usually did so only to exhort the heir, as did

19

Paris was Edward's favorite playground. The Pré-Catelan Restaurant in the Bois de Boulogne, shown here in 1909, was a meeting place for the rich, the titled, and the

A. Clements Baker of *The Illustrated Sporting and Dramatic News* in a poem entitled "Farewell":

Who loves the land, the dear old land that bore us—
Who holds her honour as no party scheme—
Who fain would front whatever lies before us,
From foes who plot or fools who only dream—
Who loves this country—for the past a debtor,

And doubtful for the future dark, unknown—
Will join the chorus—where could we do better?—
"Long may Victoria's memory guide the Throne!"

The strong current of apprehension that runs like a tide through these lucubrations sprang from a realization that for more than twenty years the Edwardians had stood in the wings of history waiting to take over their heri-

tage and enjoy it—openly, publicly, and without reproof. But Victoria had gone on year after year, as the Prince of Wales grew older and fatter, more habituated to a restless life of pleasure, and yet, quaintly enough, still very nervous in his mother's presence. The queen might stir love and devotion in her subjects, but she scared the daylights out of her children and grandchildren.

She had mothered half the mon-

demimonde: just the social pâté *Edward relished.*

archs of Europe, and now, splendiferous in uniforms of staggering grandeur, they followed on foot the tiny coffin on its flag-draped gun carriage. To the sound of rolling drums and muted fifes, it moved steadily through the complex ritual of royal death to its last resting place by the side of the endlessly mourned Prince Albert. Edward VII knew that at fifty-nine he had little time to lose. He lost none. For ten brilliant years the Edwardian age

glittered, more, alas, with tinsel than with gold, but none could deny its careless sparkle.

*E*xcluded as a boy, excluded as a young man, excluded as a mature man, and excluded in late middle age from the affairs of state, Edward VII had been free to amuse himself according to his inclinations. As regularly as the seasons he moved from the gaming tables of Marienbad and Biarritz to the racecourses of Doncaster and Ascot; during February and May he entertained, went to the theatre, and visited his female friends at five o'clock for a *thé complet*. As regularly as a migratory bird he left in March for two months in the sun; in August he was resplendent in naval gear at the Cowes Regatta, in October at Balmoral for the deer and grouse, at Christmas and the New Year—Sandringham.

Now, his ministers pursued him as best they might, inured to all-night trains, tempestuous sea passages, and the dank discomfort of Balmoral. The country's business had to go on, but at least the monarch had style, and was clearly pursuing a life that his subjects could vicariously enjoy. Queen Victoria may have had a chilling presence, innate dignity, and grandeur that derived from isolation, but there was little her subjects could participate in: a glimpse of her at the occasional jubilee or as she flashed by in the royal train. She might be a public symbol of widowhood and motherhood, but hers was a deeply lived private life. Her major palaces were moribund. Only the private houses of Osborne and Balmoral had the impress of her personality and that of her husband.

Edward gave up Osborne and refurbished the rest. He intended to live in his palaces to the full. He got special pleasure from breaking up or burying the life-sized statues of Victoria's gillie, John Brown, with whom she had shared in later middle age an occasional dram of whisky—a solecism that Edward was never likely to commit. His mistresses were pretty, elegant, witty, well-

"The Rare, the rather awful visits of Albert Edward, Prince of Wales, to Windsor Castle," runs the title of Max Beerbohm's cartoon about Victoria and her wayward son. She may not have made him stand in a corner, but Edward never lost his fear of her.

born, and usually discreet—and they knew their place. At his accession he was firmly in the hands of Mrs. George Keppel, a charming and beautiful creature of exceptional social skill, who never exploited her position. She managed even to be liked by Queen Alexandra, who invited her to share the vigil by Edward's deathbed.

*T*he king's mistress was as much a magnet as the king himself, and the pair never lacked for cronies. Their circle was at once aristocratic and rich, but it was also cosmopolitan, and what is so rare for a monarch of that date, in no way anti-Semitic, for both the Rothschilds and the Cassels were close friends. Earlier they had rescued him financially and had helped create the circumstances in which he could enjoy his extravagant life.

Sometimes Edward's entourage was referred to as "The Bodies," in contrast with the more intellectual segment of English aristocratic society led by Arthur Balfour and Margot Tennant. She married Asquith, afterward the

21

Liberal prime minister. Their circle of friends was known as "The Souls." The difference between Bodies and Souls, however, lay not so much in their sexual mores as in their social interests. The Souls loved talk—talk about politics, talk about people, talk about books, talk about the theatre. If the talk became too gossipy and private at her dinner parties, Margot Asquith would quell the table with her high, piercing voice and demand "general conversation."

Like the Bodies, the Souls maintained the code that was so much a part of the Edwardians' attitude toward life. As one of Edward's friends phrased it, "It does not matter what you do, so long as you don't frighten the horses." The public must not be shocked. If Balfour slept with Lady Elcho, she nevertheless arrived at house parties with her husband, and Balfour slipped along to her bedroom in the dark. No one acknowledged their adultery, although everyone knew of it. It was the same with the Bodies. Their relationships were passionate, but because they were less intelligent and less disciplined than the Souls, their scandals sometimes surfaced, particularly while they were waiting for the aged queen to die. After his accession to the throne Edward VII was older, discreeter, wearier, and much more firmly under the control of Mrs. Keppel.

The gyrations of these gilded creatures, whether Bodies or Souls, were noted at endless length in the social pages (not columns) of the daily press. They were perpetually photographed —at races, at the theatre, at the opera, at garden parties, and at Biarritz, Nice, or Marienbad. Their public role was similar to that of film stars in the twenties and thirties and of pop stars in the sixties. They projected an image of glamour, sophistication, and riches to the people forever denied such pleasures. As an aristocracy on constant

George Bernard Shaw (left) was photographed with H. G. Wells at a meeting of the Fabian Society before 1908, when Wells resigned.

view, they represented a curious and unique place in history. The growth of democratic attitudes had not progressed far enough for ordinary men and women to create their own heroes and heroines, except in sport or the theatre, and so they looked for glamour where it was traditionally to be found, among the titled and the rich.

The Edwardian nobility was popular with large segments of the population. The Prince of Wales's triumph with his thoroughbred Persimmon at the Derby in 1896 made the public hysterical. Photographs of his mistress Lily Langtry adorned thousands of walls. The Earl of Derby was immensely popular, as was the Earl of Lonsdale, a prize-fight enthusiast, with his yellow carriages and footmen in yellow livery. Aristocratic weddings at St. George's, Hanover Square, or at St. Margaret's, Westminster, drew crowds of thousands.

After the moral earnestness, the soul searching, and the widow gloom of the Victorian world, the pleasure-loving Edward and his friends cast a radiance over English life. Edwardian England certainly had its darker side, and it was not short of men of deep social conscience and radical intentions, but there can be no doubt that England took to play and pleasure during the

Edwardian age as it had never done before. These were the boom years of three-day cricket matches, of football, of daily race meetings, of music halls and theatres. They saw the astonishing development of the seaside resort, especially of Blackpool and Brighton, with their Coney Island fun fairs and vulgar postcards. There was on the surface a sense of ebullience and joy, which radiated from the figure of the king, small maybe, fat maybe, but dignified and with a mode all his own, from the trim of his beard to the tilt of his hat and the angle of his cigar. Like all monarchs who achieve great popularity, he possessed the delight of an actor in self-presentation and also a great actor's sense of timing. Victoria might have been more revered, but no other sovereign in modern times has won the warmth and affection of his subjects in quite the same way that Edward did.

And yet, his gilded world was something of a mirage, and even Edward's popularity sprang from the coarser, more Philistine, more thoughtless, elements of English society. The English aristocracy lived on a curious tightrope of self-deception. Their actions belied their beliefs. Only the very stupid or the very insensitive among them could have been unaware that this was so. Intelligent outsiders regarded the behavior of the rich as an outrageous hypocrisy. And in the Edwardian era we first begin to hear those voices of criticism that in the last two decades have become a deafening roar.

Of course, there had been scandals in Victoria's age, but most men in public life had attempted to live according to its harsh morality, and when they failed, some of them, like Parnell or Dilke, had their careers blighted. In Edward's England there was a conspiracy against ostracism. Arthur Balfour carried on with Lady Elcho for years and probably had a

Edwardian London's chic Bohemians usually dined at the Café Royal, shown here in a painting of 1912. Augustus John appears in the right foreground.

23

son by her; the king knew it, yet Balfour's career suffered not at all. The aristocratic whoremasters, the noble pursuers of jockeys as well as the turf, the gamblers, and for that matter, the cardsharps—all were part of that gilded world. There were even darker contrasts. The banquets, the lavish and spectacular consumption, the torrent of gold earned so easily and spent so profusely, stood out garishly against a background of poverty, low wages, and widespread malnutrition.

There had always been great tension in Victorian England, a deep concern among the sensitive about the contrast between "the dark satanic mills" and their own self-indulgent lives of elegance and refinement. A few Victorians had worried about the hypocrisy that sheathed the legs of a grand piano but did nothing about child prostitution. And from the eighteen eighties on, the most powerful voices in English intellectual life had begun to criticize their world, either directly, like George Bernard Shaw, H. G. Wells, Havelock Ellis, Edward Carpenter, and the rest, or by implication, as Oscar Wilde and his friends did in poetry, plays, and their style of life. But others, such as Yeats and his friends, retreated into the Gaelic twilight, rejecting the harsh realities of industrial England just as completely.

At Edward's accession few writers and few intellectuals took an unalloyed delight in their world. Even Kipling, the poet of the Empire, in his great poem "The Recessional," written for the queen's Diamond Jubilee in 1897, was full of foreboding, heavy with the sense of inevitable decay of empire and greatness. The Boer War divided English society in the way that Vietnam does ours. The British army singularly failed to cope with the South African guerrilla forces, com-

MARIE LLOYD

CAMILLE CLIFFORD

MARIE STUDHOLME

Corseted, befeathered, and stylishly bedecked, these ladies were stars of the Edwardian music halls. Miss Clifford was a dancing Gibson girl who gave up the stage to marry a peer of the realm.

mitting some foolish atrocities in the process, and the majority of intellectuals, writers, and artists were deeply disturbed by England's policy. The more thoughtful of them were equally shocked by the revelation that fully a third of the recruits for the British army were suffering from malnutrition.

Sensitive eyes could not fail to see the terrible contrasts in London itself—the slums of Bethnal Green, with perhaps one earth closet to a dozen families and one water faucet in the street or court for a cluster of houses; the houses themselves alive with bugs and fever; the children dirty, illiterate, unkempt, and often debauched. Yet less than three miles away was the glitter of Mayfair, the profusion of food and drink, whoring and gambling, the idle men and women drifting from one extravagant amusement to another. And the contrasts outside the metropolis of London were no less vivid and no less shocking.

Not surprisingly, the Edwardian

age developed a strong streak of middle-class socialism, exemplified by the powerful Fabian Society led by Beatrice and Sidney Webb, around whom clustered most of the intellectual aristocracy of England—Rupert Brooke, G. M. Trevelyan, and Bertrand Russell, plus Shaw, Wells, and Bennett. It started slowly in the 1880's as the Fellowship of the New Life, but by the beginning of World War I it had collected nearly four thousand members from the most influential groups—social as well as intellectual—in English life. Bertrand Russell, every inch an aristocrat, was so deeply moved by his socialist convictions that he gave away his inherited wealth and reduced himself to poverty.

Most of the Fabians were intellectual members of the middle class, and this fact has been of enduring importance in English political life, for it made socialism respectable. By giving the Labor party a considerable middle-class leadership, it helped moderate the sharp conflict between classes that the social injustices of Edwardian England were fostering. Many of the Fabians found, as Galsworthy did, that the pull of middle-class life was stronger than the pull of socialism, and so they drifted slowly back to their natural habitats; but they took with them a sense of social need and of social justice.

That politician of genius David Lloyd George, the greatest of Edwardians, realized that the growth of labor politics could only endanger the Liberal party—and in a series of masterly budgets he laid down the foundations of the welfare state upon which the Labor party was to build after World War II. Not, however, without a struggle. His measures—such as old-age pensions and national insurance to cover sickness and unemployment—stirred many aristocrats

The London Hippodrome, where acrobatic acts like this played to a packed house, was the grandest of music halls, a circus and theatre combined. The appeal of this kind of entertainment crossed class barriers: king and commoner, intellectual and simpleton—they all came to enjoy the show.

to such an unbridled rage that the House of Lords threw out his Finance Bill in 1909, precipitating a ferocious constitutional crisis that may have speeded the king's death in 1910 and did lead to the reform of the Lords in 1911. Nothing more clearly highlighted the shallow hypocrisy of Edwardian England than the bitter opposition of a man as inordinately rich as the Duke of Devonshire to the idea of an aged miner securing a pittance from the state. These internal political conflicts were intensified by the intractable question of Ireland, which teetered time and time again on the brink of civil war. And yet, in spite of the gravity of the problems that faced Parliament, there was more social experimentation and a greater flexibility and originality in politics than England had experienced in decades.

The Edwardian age was one of creative conflict. The issues ranged from the plight of women to the censorship of plays, but the burden of the conflict was the same: freedom for greater self-expression, social customs and institutions more in tune with human needs, removal of restraints and insistence on justice for all, abolition of prejudice and exposure of hypocrisy. Those comfortably entrenched in the lush pastures of privilege naturally viewed such wild goals as the thin edge of anarchism, irreligion, and pagan sexuality. The plays of Mr.

Shaw, the novels of Mr. Wells, the statues of Mr. Epstein, and the art criticism of Mr. Fry turned many a bishop, many an admiral, many a general, and almost every judge purple with fury and horror. It is hard for us to think of the Edwardian literary scene as one of immense daring, full of revolutionary attitudes in art and alive with genius of a high order. But so it was. And this cultural renaissance is only now beginning to be appreciated to the fullest measure.

Liberation was what the avant-garde intellectuals and artists were after, and they attacked where the restraints and hypocrisies were most obvious and inane. Thus, the Edwardian age heard the first clarion call for women's libera-

tion. The feminists made a double attack: first, an attempt to ease the divorce laws—in which they were aided by men—and second, a struggle to secure the vote. But there they had to fend for themselves.

The *cause célèbre* in the effort to change divorce laws was provoked by Bertrand Russell's brother, Lord Russell, who deliberately commited bigamy because he could not escape from a disastrous marriage. According to the medieval rule, he was tried by his peers in the House of Lords, found guilty, and sent to jail for three months, becoming in the process a public hero of the left. In spite of bishops, moralists, and Edward VII himself (who loathed divorce as much as he loved adultery), the liberals won, and Parliament made divorce a little more easily and cheaply obtainable, if no less squalid in its attendant publicity.

The suffragettes had a tougher fight. They chained themselves to the railings of 10 Downing Street, they went on hunger strikes in jail, and in 1913 one martyr flung herself under the galloping race horses at the Derby in the presence of King George V—all to no avail. It required the great liberator, World War I, to crack male domination in politics. Nevertheless, it was these passionate, dedicated, single-minded Edwardian women, led by Emmeline Pankhurst, who heralded the long slow revolution in the position of women that is today beginning to snowball.

A faint scent of liberty began to infuse the cultural air of Edwardian England. Like so much that flourished then, it originated in the 1880's and 1890's. Oscar Wilde, Aubrey Beardsley, and the *Yellow Book* had titillated late Victorian England with their aura of sophisticated sin. Edward Carpenter and Havelock Ellis had led an open assault on the hypocrisy of Victorian sexual attitudes, proclaiming not only that male and female homosexuality was widespread but that it was natural. This early dawn quickly

PHOTOWORLD–FPG

If Maugham (opposite) is the picture of Edwardian urbanity, here is his rural counterpart—a rifle in hand, dog at heel, cigarette at the ready—engaged in a day's shooting.

ended in disaster. Wilde went to jail; Ellis's books were suppressed; Carpenter was persecuted. Such results frightened the sinners and the sophisticated. Some crossed the Channel, and the others retreated into silence. But revival came with the new reign, and the voices for freedom were not muted for long. Two years before the king's accession Dora Kerr had published a blistering attack on England's sexual morality. Her criticism was twofold and is best expressed in her own words:

We profess ignorance in children, entire sex suppression in girls and youths, full-blossomed knowledge and wisdom at the moment of marriage, unrelieved life-long sex-starvation for half the women of the upper class, and deprivation during the most vigorous years in life of the majority of men. There is (fortunately) *some* difference between what is professed and what is actually done . . . There is a great deal of Free-Love among married people in England, in the refined classes . . . the one great drawback to it is the amount of deceit which endangers self respect.

The theme of sexual hypocrisy was taken up and developed by some of the

suffragettes, who realized that the social position of women could never be changed until men ceased to exploit them, either in marriage or prostitution. As Mrs. Pankhurst vividly phrased it, "Votes for Women and Chastity for Men." There were minor victories: an excellent birth-control manual sold merrily at fifty thousand copies a year; most barbers and some chemists were well stocked with contraceptive devices, yet were not prosecuted. A plea for the social acceptance of "bachelor mothers" led to insults for the author, but not jail. And, of course, the new woman was visible, not only in St. John's Wood among the literary and artistic Bohemians, but also on the stage and in best-selling novels. The Edwardian writers developed a new style of heroine, one who was sexually alive and sexually frank—Wells's Ann Veronica, Galsworthy's Irene Forsyte, Shaw's Major Barbara: "emancipated" was the word for them.

Creations such as these were regarded by the conservative forces with horror. The good and the fearful closed ranks. The Purity League was formed; the Mother's Union got up in arms; bishops thundered in the House of Lords; there were repeated National Councils on Public Morals; schoolmasters, led by Edward Lyttleton, headmaster of Eton, condemned adolescent sexual activity as fatal to health and morals. The Circulating Libraries Association, putting the country's salvation higher than private gain, purged their shelves of pornography and set up a personal censorship as savage and as quaint as that of the Lord Chamberlain over the theatre. Even Henry James's *Italian Hours* was banished—on some librarian's whim—and the London County Council refused to allow *Dombey and Son* to be given as a school prize. A clutch of busybodies called The Crusaders hoped to reimpose censorship by law.

But these groups were like King Canute and the tide: he could no more hold the sea back than the old guard

Looking exactly like a character in one of his own polished comedies, W. Somerset Maugham posed for this portrait, entitled The Jester, *in 1911.*

could stifle change. The stultifying and tortuous censure of the moralists was answered by some of the wittiest and most passionate writers twentieth-century England has known, who vigorously and brilliantly attacked both the official censorship on the stage and the unofficial one in the libraries. As with literature, so with art. The early impressionist shows in England in the 1880's had been greeted with bewilderment and horror. Renoir's nudes sent chills down episcopal spines. Naturally, when Roger Fry brought postimpressionist paintings to London in 1910, they were abused as the works of lunatics and psychopaths. But the French poison spread. Walter Sickert and Wilson Steer, both converts to impressionism, started the New English Art Club. George Moore, the novelist and art critic, preached the virtues not only of impressionism but also of realism and symbolism.

Members of the avant-garde attacked the Royal Academy, charging that Sir Francis Chantrey's bequest to the nation was being wasted on banal works. Almost every painter of merit, let alone of innovation, had been neglected, and the commonplace ones flattered by high prices. A first-class fight took place in the House of Lords in 1904, when Lord Lytton successfully indicted the Royal Academy and obtained a select committee to investigate the Chantrey bequest. Alas, the results were puny: the issues were evaded or swept aside, and the academicians pursued their dreary way, as they still do. But new attitudes toward art had at least been ventilated, and the self-complacency of the Establishment demonstrated. The tensions so created were to prove a wonderful stimulus to British art, which took on a vigor, a freshness, and a sense of experimentation that was wholly admirable, and was to lead to Henry Moore and Graham Sutherland.

Wherever we look—at the Empire and its fading rituals, at the condition of England, at social and political pro-

COLLECTION OF MRS. MICHAEL FOOT, COURTESY OF GEORGE RAINBIRD, LTD.

Sweet face, ribbons, and all, Emmeline Pankhurst was a militant suffragette. As founder of the Women's Social and Political Union, she was always on the march, and often in jail.

test, at the new movements in art and literature—the Edwardian age is obviously at war with itself, creating tension and strain within the growing and socially powerful classes. Although there were still myriads of self-satisfied Victorians, the more sensitive and intelligent men and women were horrified by the double standards of both life and thought.

How could one reconcile Edward VII's refusal to allow a divorced person, because convicted of adultery, into the Royal Enclosure at Ascot with the known fact that he himself was sleeping with Mrs. George Keppel? How could one reconcile the lavish dinners of a noble establishment—with course following course like a feast of Trimalchio's—with the terrible discoveries of Seebohm Rowntree that the average unskilled laborer in the town of York could not earn enough to keep his family from starvation? How could one reconcile social attitudes toward sex—repressive, terrifying, harmful—with the known facts of life and living?

John Singer Sargent's portrait (opposite) of three Edwardian beauties—the Wyndham sisters—is the image of an almost impossibly aristocratic feminine grace. Lady Elcho, later Arthur Balfour's mistress, is at far left.

How could one reconcile the availability of expensive pornography with the attempt to suppress Wells's *Ann Veronica?* How could one reconcile the lewd innuendoes of Marie Lloyd in the music halls with the banning on the stage of Shaw's *The Shewing Up of Blanco Posnet?* More and more men and women could not, and the voice of protest grew from a squeak to a roar. Nevertheless, I am sure that it was the tensions that double standards caused in private as well as in public that provided much of the creative stimulus of this great literary and artistic age.

In these years two tides met and created turbulent waters. There was the stately sweep of traditional England, concerned with preserving the old society of status and deference; for believers in this past, monarchy, church, family, and the traditional morality were as sacred as the Book of Isaiah. But the new tide was beginning to run toward its flood—mass education, almost universal literacy, growing affluence for the lower-middle class, an army of men and women who wanted not subjection and a restrictive morality but a taste of the joys that the aristocratic and wealthy Edwardians had never denied themselves.

The old world was cracking, and the new, mass consumer society, with its tensions and conflicts, its demands for innovation and change, its call for personal freedom of every kind, was beginning to seep through in an uncheckable stream. And yet there was one quality of the Edwardians that neither derived from the traditional past nor was, alas, to be typical of the future, and that was gusto. Edward VII lived as if he enjoyed every hour of every day, and so did most of his subjects; and that, perhaps, is what gives their age its present radiance.

A PORTFOLIO OF PHOTOGRAPHS BEGINS ON PAGE 32

Weekending,

The king (center) at a hunting party

Or, Why We Cannot Forgive the Edwardians

This essay first appeared in December, 1929, in Vanity Fair. *Though no Edwardian, Sir Harold had the gusto for accomplishment that characterized that period: he was a diplomat, statesman, biographer, historian, and wit. His last published works were his diaries. He died in 1968, at the age of eighty-two.*

The age of Edward VII will, we may presume, live in history as an age of comfort. *It was not.* It was an age of fevered luxury, and an age of peculiar human ineptitude. People in those Edwardian days possessed false values, and they endeavored, fortunately without success, to impose these values upon their children. The whole glittering decade—the first decade of our century—passed in an atmosphere of plethoric friction. It is time that the jade and lobster of the Edwardian epoch were exposed.

In the first place, people ate excessively, and competitively. No age since that of Nero can show such unlimited addiction to food.

A man, under King Edward, was called by his valet at eight thirty. Valets then were silent but hostile men, who would arrive bearing in their left hand a neat brass can of shaving water, and in their right hand a neat brass tray of tea, toast, and Marie biscuits. The Edwardian—his blinking, plethoric eyes above his pink silk eiderdown—would munch the biscuits and sip the tea. He would then adjust his teeth, adjust his hair, adjust his afghan dressing robe, and slouch, plethoric, along the passage to the bathroom. If he were staying from Saturday to Monday in a rich house (and all houses in the Edwardian epoch were rich), he would find in the bathroom the scented smell of his predecessor's indulgence (*fla-*cons was the word they used), which contained the *Hamam Bouquet* of Mr. Penthalicon. The guest would pour this unguent into the bath from which his valet would already have removed the stains, the soap-suds, and the other *disjecta membra* of the former occupant. The water would be tepid. Edwardian water was always tepid. His predecessor had left his signet ring in the soap dish. Through the smell of *Hamam Bouquet* would gradually pierce the smell of lavender bags and *Sanatas.* Disgusted and dyspeptic, the Edwardian would proceed with his bath. He shaved in it.

When he returned to his bedroom, along the red pile carpet which marked the unending symmetry of the corridor, he would find that the windows had been slightly opened and that his clothes had been laid ready for him upon the chintz settee. Taking a *Régie* cigarette from his *Fabergé* case, he would contemplate these clothes with satisfaction. If he were a good Edwardian, his shirt and collar would be all in one. A white shirt, somewhat frilled and tucked on the breast, ended in a stiff little upturned collar. Hard, expectant, circular—that collar would shortly encase his neck. Alternatively, a Piccadilly collar of equal rigidity would be waiting for him on the dressing table. Black clothes; a gray silk tie; a neat turquoise pin representing a pheasant walking slowly from left to right; a white cambric handkerchief; a dab of eau de cologne; his purse; his cardcase; the smell of *Euchrisma* as he brushed his hair. Then he descended, down red pile staircases, to breakfast.

Only the really improper Edwardians had breakfast in their rooms. The others met, on that Sunday morning, in the dining room. The smell of last night's port had given place to the smell of this morning's spirits of wine. Rows of little spirit lamps warmed rows of large silver dishes. On a table to the right, between the windows, were grouped Hams, Tongues, Galantines, Cold Grouse, ditto Pheasant, ditto Partridge, ditto Ptarmigan. No Edwardian meal was complete without Ptarmigan. Hot or cold. Just Ptarmigan. There would also be a little delicate rectangle of pressed beef from the shop of M. Benoist. On a further table, to the left, between the doors, stood fruits of different caliber, jugs of cold water, and jugs of lemonade. A fourth table contained the porridge utensils. A fifth, coffee, and pots of Indian and China tea. The latter were differentiated from each other by little ribbons of yellow (indicating China) and red (indicating, without *arrière-pensée,* our Indian empire). The center table, which was prepared for twenty-three people, would be bright with Malmaisons and toast racks. No newspapers were, at that stage, allowed.

The atmosphere of the Edwardian dining room at nine thirty was essentially daring. A pleasant sense of confederacy and sin hung above the smell of spirit lamps. For had they not all been brought up to attend family prayers? And had they not all eluded that obligation? It was true, of course, that the host and hostess, with their niece, had (at nine) proceeded to the family chapel and heard the butler reading a short collect for the day. But the guests had for their part evaded these Victorian obligations. This corporate evasion gave to the proceedings an atmosphere of dash. There was no insincerity in the bright gaiety with which they greeted each other, with which they discussed how he or she had slept. "A little kedgeree, Lady Maude," "Oh, thank you, Mrs. Stapleton."

Evidently it was all going very well.

Edwardian breakfasts were not a hurried proceeding. The porridge was disposed of negligently, people walking about and watching rain descend upon the Italian garden. Then would come whiting and omelette and deviled kidneys and little fishy messes in shells. And then tongue and ham and a slice of ptarmigan. And then scones and honey and marmalade. And then a little melon, and a nectarine or two, and just one or two of those delicious raspberries. The men, at that stage, would drift (I employ the accepted term) to the smoking room. The women would idle in the saloon watching rain descend upon the Italian garden. It was then ten thirty.

If the house possessed no private chapel, the guests would then "assemble in the

By HAROLD NICOLSON

hall." There would be footmen fussing about in cockaded top hats and long buff overcoats with gold buttons. A degree of jollity would be extracted from the process of deciding who would drive to church in the wagonette, who in the landau, who in the victoria, who in the brougham. And who should walk. The latter category seized umbrellas and capes. People jingled off, clasping their prayer books and the half crown for the offertory. From the side door the children, wide-eyed and washed, would appear with their governesses. They crossed the park to the church beyond the lodge.

With fervor would these Edwardians sing the hymns, with reverence would they listen to the stories from the Old Testament. The smell of leather and wet mackintosh would permeate the damp little church. Every now and then an umbrella would tumble from a pew. The final benediction descended upon rows of bowed heads. The ladies' hats were rich with artificial flowers; the heads of the men were rich with the smell of *Euchrisma.* They walked back under dripping trees.

The half hour before luncheon hung a little heavy on their hands. The women would repair to their rooms and deal with their hair and faces. The men would gather in the library, where they would shortly be joined by the curate or, as the case might be, the house chaplain. A shy little man this, not knowing all these London people, not very certain how to modulate his voice. The younger men would come in later, having changed into tweeds. There were silver vases of white roses, and cut-glass vases in which the roses were red. The hostess, passing from group to group, would flick irritable emerald-laden fingers at these flowers, tugging them into different shapes. They would pass in to luncheon. The curate, hanging behind, would hang behind.

Edwardian luncheons were strained and bright. There was a theory that the good hostess should "draw her guests into conversation." This entailed a process of flinging conversational flies across the vast table and not waiting to see if the fish rose. "Colonel Westmacott, you simply *must* tell us about the Zambesi," and "Oh, Clara! Is it *really* true that dearest Evie has got to go to Nauheim?" There was a buzz of general talk. It would only be a buzz.

After luncheon they walked around the park. They did not visit the stables. Since the introduction of motors, the stables had become Victorian. The elder members of the party would drive over to Stonehenge in an open Daimler. They appeared, aged and flustered, in motoring veils of watered

silk. Colonel Westmacott, in a tweed cape and spats, stumped off with Lady Moira to visit the quarries. Captain Fairfax took Miss Sinclair for a drive in his de Dion. Professor Steinholtz slept.

Tea was served in the blue gallery. There were little ginger biscuits, which one could only get from Biarritz and of which one kept a store in case the king came. All Edwardian houses kept stores of things like ginger biscuits and *aubergines* and French patisseries and bath salts *in case the king came.* And he did come. He came over and over again. And on Monday morning other people would read all about it in the *Morning Post.* It was only, however, when the king actually did come that one went so far as to have lobster salad for tea. Otherwise, one just had scones, and egg sandwiches, and *pâté* sandwiches, and cucumber sandwiches, and chocolate cake, and walnut cake, and coffee cake—and cake. Also there were little plates with china-handled knives to match, from which people ate *Tiptree* jam with toast or brioches. The butler, the groom of the chambers, the underbutler, and the footmen would move about offering food. But in the best houses (and most Edwardian houses were the best) the servants did not remain for tea.

After tea there would be bridge tables in the red drawing room, and the men would not infrequently play billiards. Dinner was at half past eight. The women would return an hour before to change their tea gowns for the other things which they donned to dine. The men would also change into clothes even more galling and restrictive than those they had worn all day. The guests would reassemble in the saloon.

The host by this time was already bored by his party and would indicate, a little irritably, who was to take in whom. He held a fussy little piece of paper in his hand and would fuss from one man to another. The women, one by one, entered the room slowly, showing off their clothes. Then there would be dinner. Ptarmigan and champagne. Champagne and ptarmigan. The hostess did not endeavor to stimulate general conversation at dinner. One only did that at luncheon. At dinner people talked, inclining their neat bodies, sideways, at their neighbors. At nine forty-five the women swept, with backward glances, from the room. The host would take his glass of port, holding it with gingerly fingers from above, and move to the seat vacated by his wife. At ten fifteen they joined the ladies in the music gallery.

Bridge again. And at midnight, in the Holbein room, there would be deviled chicken, and more sandwiches, and every

form of spirit and mineral water which man or woman could desire. In the corridor upstairs the ladies' maids would hang, listlessly yawning. Fires would sparkle in the grates, reflected in brass bedstead and in mirror. The pink silk reading lamps were lit beside the beds. Upon the night table stood bottles of *Malvern Water* and of *Vichy,* and covered dishes of sandwiches. A ribboned coverlet of swansdown would be draped across the sofa. The kettle, by the fireplace, purred.

Next morning the gentlemen were awakened. Their valets would pack their *Enos* and their shooting sticks. They would return by train to London. Their carriages would meet them, horses champing bits, at the arrival platform of Paddington. In the train coming up to London, the members of the house party would read, in the *Morning Post,* a list of the members of the house party. They returned to Curzon Street feeling very pleased indeed. And next Saturday it would all begin again.

Compared to the strenuous social discipline which these hardy people imposed upon themselves, our own laxity may seem a little decadent. Who among us today would really dress for church and dress for luncheon and dress for tea and dress again for dinner? Who among us would possess the endurance to relish all those meals, to relish all that tittle-tattle? Who today would care whether he was or was not invited to Upyatt Lacy or to West Warren? Who today prints or reads those lists of Saturday to Monday parties?

The war has not been fought in vain. We have been released from false pretensions. We have our jumpers, our cocktails, and our freedom. We can smoke pipes in Bond Street, and wear gray flannels in June.

I do not regret that I was old enough to touch the fringe of Edwardian luxury. But I render thanks to Providence that I was also young enough to relish and share the wider liberties of our subsequent age. Let us be frank about it. The Edwardians were vulgar to a degree. They lacked style. They possessed only the hard glitter of their own electric light: a light which beat down pitilessly upon courtier, ptarmigan, bridge scores, little enamel boxes, and plates and plates of food. They lacked simplicity, and their intricacies were expensive but futile. I, for one, prefer the wide circle of our simpler horizon.

Nor, when all is said and done, can one forgive the Edwardians for their fundamental illusion. For it never dawned upon them that intelligence was of any value.

Edwardian Exteriors

A Portfolio of Photographs

Blenheim Palace, seat of the dukes of Marlborough, was in 1896 the scene of a stiflingly magnificent house party in honor of Edward and Alexandra, then Prince and Princess of Wales. Among the guests honorable and the guests notable was Arthur Balfour (seventh from left in the back row), later prime minister. Seated, from the left, are Lord Chesterfield, Lady Randolph Churchill (mother of Winston), the Duchess of Marlborough (née Consuelo Vanderbilt), Alexandra, one Mr. H. Chaplin, and the Prince of Wales, at center. The Duke of Marlborough is seated on the grass at right. The ladies changed their elaborate dresses four times a day—never wearing the same one twice—and the party lasted from Monday to Saturday.

No stately rituals were required in this English meadow, where one Sunday afternoon in the summer these ordinary mortals picnicked on the grass. Six days'

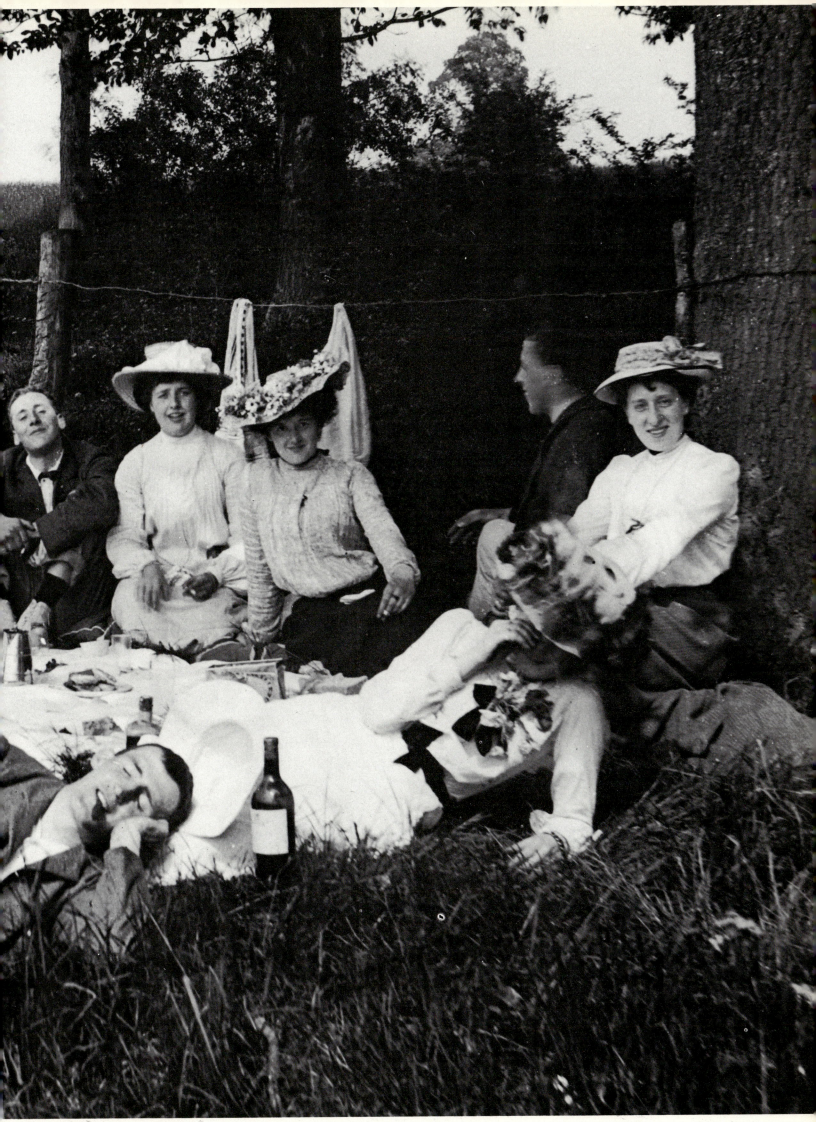

work may be behind them, and six to come; but today the fare is cake and wine. And for the moment, no Edwardian rain falls upon the Edwardian bonnets.

In London's East End in 1909 these Edwardians came out into their Stepney courtyard and were photographed. Like the picnickers on the preceding

two pages, but utterly unlike the Blenheim house guests, they are forever anonymous, it being a perquisite of wealth to have one's name remembered.

The exhausting efforts once entailed in an afternoon's pleasure may be imagined by counting heads in this picture: 27, and all servants but the woman with

a stick. She is Lady Isabella Battie-Wrightson, and she is about to serve tea for the local infantry regiment. The officers and Lady Isabella took their tea indoors.

In whatever season Edward might have died, some social event would have been blighted. As it happened, his demise threatened the opening of Ascot in June,

1910. But Ascot opened, and as a fitting memorial to the sportsman-king—and unknowingly to his era—society came to the races, as above, dressed in black.

The Mummy's Curse

The mummy, seated benignly in his London cupboard,
is Jeremy Bentham, and his curse is his mischievous
dictum: the greatest good for the greatest number

In Gower Street in London, among the gray early-nineteenth-century squares of Bloomsbury and not far from the British Museum, is University College, the oldest college of the University of London. After crossing the courtyard, past the great Corinthian portico, and turning into the main entrance hall, one finds oneself confronted, at the far end on the right, by what appears to be a large and rather handsome clothes cupboard. Lettered in gilt across the top are the words JEREMY BENTHAM. It is, in fact, a bald and entirely accurate description of the contents. For when the doors are opened, one indeed finds, screened by a pane of glass, Jeremy Bentham—legal philosopher, reformer, oracle, and sage to many influential disciples in all parts of the world—who died a hundred and thirty-nine years ago. His garments drab with age, he sits, in the manner he himself directed, as though poised to write one of those characteristic sentences, original in content but grammatically a calculated assault upon the English language, that appear so frequently in the vast piles of Bentham manuscripts housed in another part of the college.

Almost a century and a half after his death Jeremy Bentham lingers on in the discreetly clothed flesh. The head that hatched utilitarianism has been replaced by a wax one.

In only one respect is his "Auto-Icon," as Bentham called this bizarre legacy of himself, inauthentic: the head, with its aged broad-brimmed hat and mild, benign half-smile, is a wax replica. The actual head, after resting a trifle obscenely for a while at Bentham's feet, is now housed on a shelf above, in a box rather like a large tea caddy. Bentham, in the clause of his will that provided instructions for this disposal of himself, added the slightly macabre wish that if his friends should care to hold gatherings to honor the memory of the founder of the "philosophy of utility," he might be physically present.

There is a literalness about all this—a desire always to evoke the concrete nub of the matter, leaving as little as possible to the imagination—that is typical of Bentham's thought. He once observed it was a pity the apple that had supposedly suggested to Newton the idea of gravitation had not been preserved in a glass case. He himself, who had written of his aspiration to be the Newton of legislation, was to miss no such opportunity: *si monumentum requiris*—if you are seeking a memorial . . . open the cupboard doors.

It would be false and ungenerous, however, to imply that Bentham's real legacy could be confined within a nicely polished wooden box. When he died in 1832, just two days before the passage of the great Reform Act enlarging the franchise for which he and his followers had worked, his name was already both revered and controversial. For the greater part of his long life he had worked with little recognition, covering endless sheets of paper with diverse and often uncompleted projects that were written, in his later years, in an increasingly obscure and uncouth jargon of his own perverse creation. It was a style that led the critic William Hazlitt to remark that, Bentham's works having been translated into French, they should now be translated into English.

Bentham must often have seemed merely a gifted crank, obsessively toiling over tasks doomed to remain unfinished and unappreciated. Apart from what was, in a sense, the central work of his life, a new constitutional code, there were plans for a model prison, perpetual peace, and a new universal grammar; long essays and pamphlets on economics, education, the poor law, usury, and rules of evidence; and radical and anticlerical tracts. Much of this mass is still unpublished, but the doyen of Bentham scholarship, Charles W. Everett, has estimated the total quantity to be some twenty million words. Bentham was, in some ways, the archetype of the unrecognized inventor, though his practical inventions were only a side line. He slept in a sleeping bag of his own design, experimented with refrigeration, and drew up projects for a harpsichord, speaking tubes, and a canal in Central America. But it was his work on the reconstruction of law and institutions that remained his abiding passion.

He eventually achieved a partial reward. Bentham lived to the age of eighty-four, and in the last two decades of his life he acquired a measure of recognition and a devoted band of disciples who proclaimed his philosophy and made it a vital and highly influential element in the great movement of reform that culminated in the early 1830's. Abroad, he became famous from Russia to South America, a revered father-figure for liberals in all parts of the world. "His name," Hazlitt wrote, slightly exaggerating the contrast for rhetorical effect, "is little known in England, better in Europe, best of all in the plains of Chili and the mines of Mexico. He has offered constitutions for the New World, and legislated for future times." John Stuart Mill, the eldest son of Bentham's chief disciple, James Mill, bracketed Bentham and Samuel Taylor Coleridge as "the two great seminal minds of England in their age," and went on to say that "there is hardly to be found in England an individual of any importance in the world of mind, who . . . did not first learn to think from one of these two."

In his earlier years Bentham had been a friend of the Whig prime minister Lord Shelburne; he had corresponded with the French revolutionary statesman Mirabeau and with the Autocrat of all the Russias, Catherine the Great. But it was in his later years, through a superficially drab group of younger followers, middle-class journalists, and educated artisans, that the influence of Bentham's ideas made itself felt: men like the dour Scotsman James Mill, the intellectual mastermind of the radical party, and his brilliant son John Stuart Mill, one of the

mentors of the Victorian age. Other disciples included the historian George Grote and the jurist John Austin, key figures in the new London University; radical politicians and agitators like John Arthur Roebuck, Joseph Hume, and Francis Place; and Edwin Chadwick, the great pioneer of public health and the poor law, who had been Bentham's secretary. Limited and philistine though some of them were, gray and forbidding though their creed often seemed to more impulsive and emotional natures (Thomas Carlyle called Benthamite utilitarianism "pig-philosophy"), these men were among the makers of Victorian England.

There were wide differences of temperament among them, but to outsiders they often seemed to be simply members of a new, aggressive, doctrinaire sect, whose points of similarity merged into a single caricature: the Utilitarian. Charles Dickens drew an unforgettable picture of one in the character of Mr. Gradgrind. The Benthamite utilitarian, seen in this light, was a bloodless calculator, intent on reducing the richness and complexity of human life and human feelings to "Mr. Bentham's oracles of utility," remorselessly processing such intangibles as pity, sentiment, beauty, and poetry through a kind of intellectual machine called "utilitarian philosophy" and coldly evaluating the results. He was a stony-faced philistine who turned men's moral and emotional life into a sort of double-entry bookkeeping of profit and loss, pleasure and pain. Some of the accusations were even contradictory. Thus, the Benthamite was both a doctrinaire man of theories and abstractions and a crass materialist who could appreciate nothing but hard facts and crude satisfactions. It would not be too difficult to find evidence to substantiate these charges, although they do not really apply to any single member of the group.

There was also, however, a natural tendency to identify this collective portrait with the founder himself and to identify the word "Benthamite" with

the man Bentham. To Karl Marx, for example, Bentham was the epitome of the narrow-minded bourgeois intellectual, the English shopkeeper turned philosopher: "the arch-philistine Jeremy Bentham, the insipid pedantic leather tongued oracle of the commonplace bourgeois intelligence of the nineteenth century." To Hazlitt he was a benign freak, a comically impractical enthusiast with no experience of life.

Hazlitt was a dramatic critic, and he presented Bentham like some old character actor's stock notion of "the philosopher." "He has lived for the last forty years in a house in Westminster, overlooking the Park, like an anchoret in his cell, reducing law to a system, and the mind of man to a machine . . . He regards the people about him no more than the flies of a summer. He meditates the coming age. He hears and sees only what suits his purpose, or some 'foregone conclusion,' and looks out for facts and passing occurrences in order to put them into his logical machinery and grind them into the dust and powder of some subtle theory."

The members of the Benthamite school contributed to this picture. Francis Place said he was as "simple as a child." The young John Stuart Mill, in revolt against the narrowness of his upbringing, wrote, rather recklessly, of him he had known personally only as an old man: "He had neither internal experience nor external; the quiet, even tenor of his life, and his healthiness of mind, conspired to exclude him from both. He never knew prosperity and adversity, passion nor satiety; he never had even the experiences which sickness gives; he lived from childhood to the age of eighty-five in boyish health. He never felt life a sore and weary burthen. He was a boy to the last."

How much truth is there in this portrait of an elderly bachelor by a brilliant but discontented younger man? Was Bentham a half-man, a stranger to all but a fragment of the full range of human passions and experience, a benevolent calculating machine? Was he really benevolent? (Even this has had doubts cast upon it.) We shall never get a final answer. But it is at least clear that Mill's portrait is overdrawn. For a fuller understanding of him, we must turn from the old Bentham to the young one, to the Bentham whom Mill did not personally know.

Jeremy Bentham was born in 1748, in Houndsditch, London, the son of a prosperous businessman. Undersized and weakly, but intellectually precocious, he was sent by his father to Oxford at the age of twelve. There, set apart from his fellows by his youth, he found little that appealed to him except a portion of the instruction in logic. He also endured an experience he never forgot: like all members of the university at the time, he had to affirm his adherence to the Thirty-nine Articles of Religion required by the Church of England. Unbelieving, Bentham did so with a passionate shame and resentment that left him lastingly embittered against both the clergy and judicial formalities.

After Oxford he became a student of law at the Inns of Court and met another disillusionment, for the law, like the universities, was passing through a period of decadence. The English lawyer's love of precedent and judge-made law, and his dislike of rigid systematization and the constricting logic of a legal code, had been carried to extreme lengths. By the late eighteenth century this had produced a situation approaching total chaos, a tangle of unsystematically related branches of law, of precedent piled on precedent, often contradictory, of gross anomalies and absurd legal fictions. To be able to pick one's way through even a part of this unpruned jungle required an erudition as profound as it was pointless for any purpose except to make the law profitable to lawyers, slow in operation, inequitable in its results, and totally incomprehensible to the unfortunate layman who became enmeshed in it. In criminal law callous injustice was sup-plemented by brutal atrocity—men were hanged, and women still sometimes burned, for trivial offenses, while graver ones carried lighter sentences.

Such was the system whose operation the young Bentham set out to study by attendance at the courts held in Westminster Hall, the great medieval hall outside the houses of Parliament, where Charles I had been tried and where England monarchs still lie in state before their funerals. In Bentham's mature philosophy he would attempt to reconstruct men's habits of moral judgment—taking nothing on trust, allowing no appeal to habit, however ingrained, or sentiment, however profound, devising a new set of rules, a new language virtually, for legislative and judicial procedure and for moral appraisal. If there seems at times to be something almost maniacal about the sheer comprehensiveness of this program, something blatantly unrealistic about the determination to undercut everything habitual and historically given, one has only to remember that Bentham as a young man had closely observed a system in which men's ordinary moral habits and sentiments had become warped by tradition and blind respect for precedent.

Yet, it was in the heart of this chaos that Bentham found his vocation. The law was a snare of unco-ordinated precedents; he would be for system and codification. The law was incomprehensible; he would devise a legal language, and a legal system, that was comprehensible even to the layman. The law was riddled with fictions, whereby things were described as something they manifestly were not; he would be against all fictions—in law, in morals, and in politics. The law was full of arbitrary, burdensome, and useless procedural rules and rituals; he would bring everything, in law and in life, to the test of its usefulness. "And have I indeed a genius for legislation?" he wrote. "I gave myself the answer, fearfully and trembling—Yes!"

Bentham knew he would never practice the law as it then existed. Such impracticality had its price; when he fell in love with a girl more than ten years younger than himself and wished to marry her, his ambitious father was unsympathetic. Bentham's worldly prospects were not good, the girl became impatient, and the affair fizzled out. Bentham remained a bachelor, and became a critic, a reformer, a would-be legislator, and the founder of a truly scientific jurisprudence.

In contrast to the archaic muddle of English law, Bentham had three main resources. The first was his own sense of equity and a cast of mind both orderly and systematic, even to excess. At Oxford he had discovered an aptitude for logic; he always liked to order and arrange, to group into classes and subclasses, to define, and then to define the elements of the definition, in a kind of bureaucracy of the intellect. The second was a hobby in which he found an order and precision that his profession so significantly lacked. He had always had a bent for science and technology; now he performed physical and chemical experiments in his lawyer's chambers and corresponded with the eminent chemist Joseph Priestley. The third resource was the self-consciously enlightened philosophy of eighteenth-century Europe, which for Bentham combined intellectual system with philanthropic purpose. In the writings of philosophers and psychologists working within the theory of knowledge established in the seventeenth century by Locke, he found the notion that all complex ideas arise from sense experiences; if our concepts are not simply meaningless words and rhetoric, they must be reducible to terms referring to our sensations.

The complexity of human motives, Bentham came to think, could similarly be resolved into two basic drives: the desire for pleasure and the avoidance of pain. The French philosopher Helvétius and the Italian jurist Beccaria had suggested how these ideas might be applied to devising a science of legislation and punishment, with the pains imposed by legal penalties nicely judged to provide just the right amount of disincentive for the various forms of antisocial behavior. From the philosophical writings of the Englishman Priestley, Bentham took the formula that for him expressed the end to be sought in every action: the greatest happiness of the greatest number. It was a discovery that evoked from him Archimedes' cry: "Eureka!"

Henceforth, everything must be brought to the judgment of this test. There was no law, no punishment, no action good or bad in its very nature; it was made so only by its consequences, measured by the standard of the "principle of utility." Legal codes, governmental institutions, prisons, schools, the moral judgments of mankind—all must be reorganized in accordance with this central idea. It would be pointless, he held, for the moralist to wish men to desire something other than pleasure, or to want "higher" pleasures than those they now want. There are no higher or lower pleasures, for this introduces an arbitrary and personal standard of judgment: "Pleasure for pleasure, push-pin is as good as poetry." Since pleasure is what all men want, no pleasure is bad in itself.

So far, this sounds like a recipe for universal permissiveness and anarchy. But there is *one* standard for judging between rival pleasures that is not arbitrary—that is a necessary consequence of deciding that pleasures or happiness is what is good and to be sought. This is *quantity* of pleasure. It would be irrational, if pleasure was the only good, not to esteem a greater quantity of pleasure more than a lesser one, and not to discourage or prohibit pleasures that, though good in themselves, ultimately caused an amount of pain outweighing the pleasure.

Bentham, in what he called his "Felicific Calculus," tried to devise ways of measuring pleasure by such qualities as certainty, intensity, duration, and so forth. All pleasures, for Bentham, were innocent until proven guilty by their consequences, however unsavory their traditional reputation. He pointed out that we only use words like "lust" and "avarice" when we have already decided that the consequences of these motives are bad; the neutral terms are "sexual desire" and "desire for gain." But an action or institution that failed, when all the calculations had been made, to come out on the plus, or "pleasure," side of the ledger was useless or pernicious, and should be prohibited or abolished. He took into account, of course, the fact that legal prohibition, backed by punishment, was itself the infliction or threat of a pain, and hence, always an evil and justified only by the prevention of a greater evil.

Bentham published these ideas in 1789 in his chief theoretical work, *An Introduction to the Principles of Morals and Legislation.* But the path to practical reform proved a long and weary one. The outbreak of the French Revolution, and the Reign of Terror, made reforming ideas suspect among the English governing class. Bentham himself allowed his time and energies to be dispersed among a number of different projects. Among them was one that absorbed the personal fortune he had inherited from his father and gave him the severest disappointments of his life. This was a project that became for a number of years an overriding obsession: the panopticon. The name derives from the Greek, meaning "all-seeing," and it was a plan for a model prison, which was later also adapted to the purposes of a paupers' workhouse. The original idea seems to have come from Bentham's brother Samuel, a naval engineer, and Bentham saw in it a remedy for the prison conditions that had already become a scandal in the late eighteenth century. In the jails of the period, scenes of Hogarthian squalor were normal. Prisoners—men, women, and children—were herded together in stench and filth, without discipline or supervision. The jailers were corrupt, and the jails formed a concentrated, exaggerated image of the world beyond their walls: the poor starved and the rich lived high, if disease did not take them, for jail fever struck down lawyers and judges as well as prisoners.

Bentham's panopticon was to be an antiseptic place of silence and order and industry and minute supervision. The world of Hogarth was to give way to the world of the laboratory mouse. The building was to be circular, with the cells around the periphery; at the center, like a spider in its web, stood the jailer. By a special arrangement of slats, he would be able to observe every cell while himself remaining invisible, communicating with the inmates by a system of speaking tubes. All the squalor and disorder and overcrowding, the rioting and vice of the existing system, were to be replaced by a healthy, centrally heated, silent penal utopia, from which human viciousness, human contact, and human warmth were alike eliminated.

Perhaps the most remarkable feature was that the system was to be run by private contract, and as the contractor Bentham proposed—himself. For years he pressed his scheme, against all criticism, on a reluctant government. He sank his fortune into the purchase of land for the project. The great antislavery reformer William Wilberforce reported seeing Bentham with tears running down his cheeks in frustration and bitterness at the government's indifference. It is little wonder that in later years he did not care to bring up the memory of his panopticon: "it is like opening a drawer where devils are locked up."

Eventually, in 1813, Bentham's personal situation was restored by substantial government compensation. The ensuing years, as the admired head of a growing band of followers, seem to have been the happiest of his life. The disappointed man of Wilberforce's description gave way to the blithe old boy of John Stuart Mill's. In his bachelor comfort he became the benevolent eccentric of the legend, making little jokes, singing little songs (he was always devoted to music, especially

Handel), fussing over his small domestic rituals, and endlessly writing. He was fond of animals, particularly "pusses and mouses," and gave pet names to his household possessions. The teapot was Dick, or Dicky. "Has my Dick begun his song?" he would ask. And when duly boiling: "Take down Dicky; he is in a passion."

Whether one finds this endearing, harmless, or repellent is, perhaps, a clue to one's attitude toward Bentham and Benthamism in general. There will never be a unanimous verdict on either. For to define one's reactions to Bentham involves reference to a set of dichotomies in human life that are as basic as the distinction between light and dark, or between hot and cold: logic versus sentiment; facts versus imagination; rationalization and system versus habit and tradition; calculation versus impulse. Most men would be willing to admit the necessity for both in some measure. But the case of Bentham, who observed that "all poetry is misrepresentation," seems to force one to a choice.

To his critics Bentham is a man who erected his limitations into a system, as John Stuart Mill implied. All his life Bentham was frightened—quite literally—of ghosts, and he connected this fear with his hatred of vague abstractions in moral and political philosophy. Knowing this, it is tempting to see something obsessive in his search for clarity and order.

But at what cost? Traditionalists and existentialists, Marxists and aesthetes, find it hard to say much good of Bentham. And he is hardly likely to become a cult figure for the young. Others find him more sympathetic. He was not strictly a behaviorist, but behaviorist psychologists find him a kindred spirit, as do logical positivists and social scientists interested in game-theory models. Logicians and philosophical jurists can admire his subtle and penetrating exploration of the logic of commands and the elegance of his principles of legal codification. Criminologists now generally share his emphasis on deterrence and reformation rather than retribution for its own sake.

But as a moral and political philosopher Bentham continues to arouse not merely specific criticisms of his logical deficiences but also a certain pervasive uneasiness. This uneasiness has been strikingly crystallized by Gertrude Himmelfarb in a recent essay on the panopticon. Bentham's model prison emerges as a nightmarish image of his own mind, of a desire to retreat into a perfectly ordered, insulated world, in which he would assume, at its center, the omnipotence and the omniscience —and the invisibility—of God. The totalitarian parallel is too close for comfort, and at the heart of the system there seems to be a kind of fear.

All pleasures, in themselves, are desirable. This Benthamite principle could be a motto for a hippie commune. But it is not only Bentham's emphasis on calculation, his denigration of impulse and neglect of spontaneity, that set him apart from such a context. It is true that there is a strong libertarian and equalitarian strain in Bentham's thought; all pleasures are good and all are equal—except in quantity. But liberty is not a good in itself; it is only a means to good, which is pleasure, or the maximization of happiness. Bentham generally endorsed private judgment as a more efficient means than government action, just as he generally endorsed private property rather than large-scale expropriation. But these principles are not intrinsic to the utilitarian position. They are not conceded as rights but adopted as means.

The possibilities of conditioning human beings, stressed by Helvétius, is not ignored by Bentham, though generally, it is true, he displays an agreeably libertarian concern for getting people the maximum amount of what they actually like, rather than with getting them to like the maximum amount of what they are actually getting. Nevertheless, there is no defense in Benthamite principles against the benevolent despot who wants to make men happy by placing a drug in the water supply or electrodes in the brain, provided he takes the trouble to do it efficiently. The examples were unknown to Bentham, but the spirit was not altogether so. "Call them soldiers, call them monks, call them machines," he wrote, "so they were but happy ones, I should not care."

The vague terms that Bentham despised and tried to eliminate, terms like human rights and human dignity, are in some respects, it seems, a better defense of what most of us think of as our interests and our humanity than Benthamite utilitarianism is. To see other people and ourselves essentially as potential recipients of stimuli, pleasant or painful, has a kind of impartiality that can on occasion be a salutary dissolvent of prejudice, but if systematized into a view and a rule of life, can become impoverishing and even sinister. The limits of my language, Wittgenstein said, are the limits of my world, and Bentham's language, in his search for concreteness and precision and system, became increasingly like the Newspeak of George Orwell's *1984*.

Our ordinary language, in its vagueness and imprecision, with its load of often unacknowledged prejudices, reflects and accommodates a diversity of values and ways of living. It is, therefore, richer in possibilities than a language tailored to the requirements of a theoretical consistency. The latter is useful in specific and limited contexts, where precision is required above all; generalized, it can become uncomfortably like a prison. It can be argued that it is with just such a specialized field—law—that Bentham was chiefly concerned. But his aspirations were wider. "We shall for we will," he wrote to his French translator Étienne Dumont, "be despots of the moral world." It was a figure of speech, but figures of speech are sometimes significant.

By Benthamite standards the British historian J. W. Burrow is highly useful to HORIZON, *which has published articles by him on Marx, Darwin, and the anarchists.*

FONS VAN WOERKOM

Are we ready for an American Lenin?

Or a Mao? Or even a Gandhi? No, argues our author—not until
"Make love, not war" gives way to "Make revolution, not love"

Many people assert that a revolutionary situation now exists in America. The nature of this supposedly impending revolution, however, is rarely discussed in depth. Only Herbert Marcuse seems to have fully confronted the differences between what he calls the Aesthetic Revolution and what I shall call the Ascetic Revolution.

The Aesthetic Revolution, already upon us, involves a rejection of the so-called Puritan ethic, with its demand for hard work, restraint of impulse, deferral of gratification, and general self-control. A possessor of these former virtues is now looked upon as being up-tight; hippie and television advertiser alike exhort us to take our pleasures now and pay later, if at all.

Behind these exhortations, of course, is a real revolution: the Keynesian Revolution. The Keynesians pioneered the transition from production to consumption values, from the Puritanical Society to the Affluent Society. They shifted saving from the balance column of virtues to that of vices, and equated deferral of gratification with a lag in the utilization of productive resources.

The Aesthetic Revolution, with its removal of repressions and controls in sex, dress, manners, and before long, perhaps, drugs, is merely the public expression of a long-term secular development. Its front-runners are the young people, especially the more affluent ones in the colleges, who have fashioned what they proudly proclaim to be a new "life style" (as opposed to the old-fashioned "way of life"). Frequently, it is these same exponents of the Aesthetic Revolution who wish to bring about a radical political and economic revolution.

This raises the possibility of a paradox. Most successful revolutions have been led by "ascetic revolutionaries," men and women who have put behind them the lures of the flesh and the attractions of the sensual. And, up to now, efforts to combine the aesthetic and the political revolutionary impulses have not worked for long.

Why? What are the characteristics of an ascetic revolutionary? Will such people emerge in America?

The ascetic revolutionary exhibits two notable traits: he manifests, or is imputed to manifest, great self-control, which entitles him to control other people; and he is unusually "free of libidinal ties," that is, he loves "no one but himself, or other people only in so far as they served his needs" (to use Freud's formulation), which allows him to pursue his revolutionary aims without sentimental weaknesses. The ideal ascetic revolutionary controls his appetites for wine, women, and song. He is, like Robespierre, incorruptible. As such, he is perceived by his followers as being without self-love or self-interest, and consequently, able to judge impartially the competing claims of others.

Moreover, like the religious martyrs, the ascetic revolutionary seems to gain a victory over the rest of us by his denial of impulse and his consequent "suffering." He conceives his right to rule as a duty imposed upon himself, rather than as an indulgence of a desire to rule. After all, has he not repressed all desire in his personal life? And this view of himself is the one he then imposes upon the rest of us. Further, his claim to rule is almost always exercised in the name of God or the general will, hence, selflessly and as a duty. Asceticism justifies the revolutionary leader to himself, and allows him to rule, and if necessary, to kill, with a clear conscience.

Many observers have commented that revolutions "cannot be made with kid gloves." Stendhal expresses this notion in *The Red and the Black*: the revolutionary must be hard, devoid of feelings, else how can he bring himself to do the terrible things necessary for the success of the revolution? It is, I suggest, by the denial of all libidinal feelings toward persons that the revolutionary steels himself for the struggle.

Any revolutionary leader is vulnerable if he has loved ones. In czarist Russia suspected Social Democrats

By BRUCE MAZLISH

> Almost always, the revolutionary
> who loves Humanity cannot abide its visible
> representatives. It is as if he
> loved Humanity because he hated human beings.

were constantly exiled and torn away from their wives; their children were hostages to fortune. The dedicated revolutionary learned quickly that he must not allow himself to be caught up in emotional ties of a family nature.

A professional revolutionary simply has no time for ordinary family concerns. At all hours he is devoted to the revolution, and when other men have gone home to their wives and children, he is still making speeches and organizing supporters. How, then, can he "love" in the ordinary manner? In some ways, he is like the man in the free-enterprise system whose whole life is his business activity, with little time or emotion left over for his family.

Yet, the revolutionary is not devoid of feelings. He does love (and hate). He loves an abstraction: Humanity, or The People, or The Proletariat. He will spend years in prison or sacrifice his life for this loved object. And his love is total, and totally positive. All good feelings are concentrated on the beloved abstraction, and all bad feelings on whoever or whatever is in opposition to it.

Real people, however, are another matter. Almost always, the revolutionary who loves Humanity cannot abide its visible representatives. It is as if he loved Humanity because he hated human beings. The French revolutionary Barras tells of a visit to Robespierre and his *gaffe* in addressing him by the familiar *tu*, used among themselves by the old revolutionaries, instead of the formal *vous*. Correcting the error failed to mollify Robespierre, who "did not betray the slightest sign of satisfaction at this sign of deference . . . I

never saw anything so impassive, either in the icy marble of statues or in the faces of the buried dead."

Not only friends, of course, but also family must be rejected by the ascetic revolutionary. Existing family relations, and the ties binding an individual to them, must be ruthlessly broken. As Hegel pointed out, it was an early revolutionary, Christ, who first exhorted his disciples to "Follow me, and forsake thy father and mother"—and himself set the example. In our time, it is a revolutionary such as Mao Tse-tung who takes up the refrain, telling his followers to abjure their family ties and relate only to him and the party.

The revolutionary leader tends to reject the rest of his past as well. To symbolize the break, he frequently takes a new name or form of address: Citizen Robespierre; Lenin instead of Ulyanov; Stalin for Dzhugashvili. If he comes from the aristocracy or the middle class, as he generally does, the ascetic revolutionary looks back with guilt on the softness and exploitiveness of his earlier existence; he aspires to become a "new man."

The prototype of this new man was a Russian populist of the 1860's, Chernyshevsky, who not only coined the phrase but served as the model for Lenin. Here is a typical description of Chernyshevsky by the historian Isaiah Berlin: "[His] harsh, flat, dull, humourless, grating sentences . . . his self-discipline, his passionate dedication to the material or moral good of his fellow man, the grey self-effacing personality, the tireless, devoted, minute industry, the hatred of style or of any concessions to the graces, the un-

questionable sincerity, the combination of brutal directness, utter self-forgetfulness, indifference to the claims of private life, innocence, personal kindness, pedantry, moral charm, capacity for self-sacrifice, created the image that later became the prototype of the Russian revolutionary hero and martyr."

In his novel, *What Is To Be Done* (1863), Chernyshevsky hailed the new man, who, like himself, was to be hard, without feelings, distrustful of sentiment, and scornful of spontaneity. By rejecting libidinal ties and practicing the ascetic virtues, he would have the requisite strength to make a revolution; he would be able to pay the necessary price for the purchase of revolutionary leadership.

Obviously, no single individual will perfectly epitomize the new man, the ascetic revolutionary. Nor will all revolutionaries be ascetics. But it is extraordinary how close the great revolutionary leaders, such as Lenin, Gandhi, and Mao, have come to the ideal type. Lenin, above all, serves as a prototype.

According to most accounts, it was the execution in 1887 of his brother Sasha, who had tried to assassinate the czar, that turned the sixteen-year-old Lenin into a full-fledged revolutionary —that and the desertion of his family at the time by their liberal friends. Lenin came to hate liberals and what he considered to be their weak, flaccid commitment to social justice.

Shortly thereafter, he found himself in trouble with the authorities, for his presence at a university protest meeting, and was rusticated to his mother's

Lenin came to exercise enormous control
over his emotions. He spurned all signs of softness
and spontaneity. Even his marriage
was a "revolutionary" one to a fellow conspirator.

estate, where he spent a year reading intensively. Chernyshevsky's ideas gripped his imagination, and provided him with an intellectual model to match the emotion aroused by his brother's death. From then on, Lenin thought of himself as a professional revolutionary, and what is more to the point, assumed the character of an ascetic revolutionary.

Certain of Lenin's traits illustrate this clearly. Compulsively thorough and fastidious, he was, as one friend put it, "order and neatness incarnate." His energy and working habits became legendary. Always his watchword was discipline, and later he was to extol the factory system for bringing discipline to the worker. In the factory, time was to be regulated closely, and Lenin was very much in character when he embraced the capitalist time-and-motion studies of Frederick Winslow Taylor, the father of scientific management, and imposed them on the Soviet workers.

Any pleasure that stood in the way of work must be given up, and Lenin showed the way. He loved chess but eventually stopped playing, for, he said, "Chess gets hold of you too much, and hinders work." So, too, with skating. He told Krupskaya, his wife, "When I was a schoolboy I used to go in for skating, but I found that it tired me so that I always wanted to go to sleep afterwards. This hindered my studies. So I gave up skating." Presumably for similar reasons, Lenin also gave up drinking and smoking.

On the positive side he disciplined himself through physical education. "You must value and take care of your health," Lenin advised a comrade. "It

is always a blessing to be physically strong and healthy, to have powers of endurance—but for the revolutionary it is a duty." Hence, play became a form of work. As Lenin's friend Gorky summed him up, "By nature he is a puritan."

Lenin came to exercise enormous control over his emotions. He spurned all signs of softness and spontaneity. Even his marriage was a "revolutionary" one to a fellow conspirator. Krupskaya, in fact, was a revolutionary companion rather than an object of romantic love. She shared his exile and served him faithfully in the cause to which they were both dedicated. There were, however, no children. One friend, perhaps nastily, described her as an "unfeminine woman," but, then, she was the "new woman" that Chernyshevsky had called for.

Two incidents dramatically illustrate Lenin's efforts to free himself from libidinal ties. The first occurred around 1900 and involved Plekhanov, Lenin's revered mentor in Marxism. In a power struggle over *Iskra,* the periodical inspired by Lenin, the younger man came to feel himself betrayed by the older, to whom he had given his devotion. We catch the flavor of Lenin's feelings, even after many years, in an emotional account of the affair called "How The 'Spark' [*Iskra*] Was Nearly Extinguished":

My infatuation with Plekhanov disappeared as if by magic, and I felt offended and embittered to an unbelievable degree. Never, never in my life, had I regarded any man with such sincere respect and veneration, never had I stood before any man so humbly and never before had I been so

brutally "kicked" . . . We [Lenin and his supporters in the power struggle] had received the most bitter lesson of our lives, a painfully bitter, painfully brutal lesson. Young comrades "court" an elder comrade out of the great love they bear for him— and suddenly he injects into this love an atmosphere of intrigue, compelling them to feel, not as younger brothers, but as fools to be led by the nose, as pawns to be moved about at will, and, still worse, as clumsy *Streber* [careerists] who must be thoroughly frightened and quashed! An enamoured youth receives from the object of his love a bitter lesson: to regard all persons "without sentiment"; to keep a stone in one's sling.

As a defense against thwarted "great love," Lenin turned to repression; henceforth, he would be "without sentiment." Significantly, soon after this episode he began to sign his articles in *Iskra* with a pseudonym: the Ulyanov given to sentiment was replaced by the unloving and unyielding Lenin. Thereafter, he had no masters and no brothers. By 1903 he had stopped addressing Martov, the closest friend of his youth, in the familiar "thou" form and had announced, "Don't look at Martov in the old way. The friendship has ended. Down with any softness."

The second incident illustrating Lenin's denial of libidinal feelings involves his reaction to music. Lenin associated music with his family; as a child he had listened for hours to his mother playing the piano. Later, he became enormously ambivalent in his reaction to music. "One evening in Moscow," Gorky relates, "when Lenin was listening to Beethoven sonatas . . . he said: 'I know nothing greater than the Appassionata, I'd like to listen to it everyday. It's beautiful, super-human music. I al-

It was Lenin's hardness, his character
as an ascetic revolutionary, that to a significant extent
attracted his small group of fellow
conspirators and propelled this extraordinary minority into
the highest authority over a huge land.

ways think proudly—it may be naive —what marvelous things people can do . . . But I can't listen to music too often, it affects the nerves, makes you want to say kind, silly things, to stroke the heads of the people who, living in a terrible hell, can create such beauty. Nowadays you mustn't stroke anyone's head, you'd get your hand bitten off, you've got to hit them over their heads, without mercy, although, ideally, we're against the use of force. H'm, h'm, our duty is infernally hard!'"

Once again we have Lenin wishing to give way to libidinal feelings but afraid of being hurt if he does, and therefore repressing his softer emotions. The political consequences of this manifested themselves, at about the time of the break with Plekhanov, in Lenin's conception of a party: the Bolshevik party. In 1902 he wrote a pamphlet, "What Is To Be Done" (borrowing the title from Chernyshevsky), that called for a party of dedicated professional revolutionaries. Their activities were to be conspiratorial rather than open, distrustful of all alliances rather than part of a general Social Democratic movement. Spontaneity and softness—these were the vices against which Lenin railed.

Then, in 1903, Lenin implemented his ideas by splitting the Russian Social Democratic party into Bolsheviks and Mensheviks, or "hards" and "softs." The consequences of this schism, a characterological as well as ideological division, are too well known to require further comment. World War I, and chance, gave Lenin his opportunity: he set about shaping a Soviet Union in his own image.

It was Lenin's hardness, his character as an ascetic revolutionary, that to a significant extent attracted his small group of fellow conspirators and propelled this extraordinary minority into the highest authority over a huge land. Lenin and his character were essential. As one scholar states categorically, "Bolshevism without him was unimaginable."

Lenin's denial of his libidinal feelings, and his submergence of them in his "hard" political party—centralized, disciplined, and dictatorial—were secured at a great emotional price. His love affair with Inessa Armand, long hidden from us by Soviet hagiology, shows this dramatically. Krupskaya, like the new woman she was, accepted the liaison, which became a triangular relationship, in good grace. Inessa reawakened Lenin's tender feelings; she radiated "warmth and ardor," we are told—by Krupskaya—and in a striking recapitulation of earlier experiences, played the piano for him. For her alone, together with his immediate family, Lenin reserved the "thou" form of address. Yet here, too, duty came before love, and for most of their relationship Lenin treated her primarily as a revolutionary companion, dispatching her on party missions and lecturing her on correct ideology. Only at her burial in 1921 did Lenin break down and exhibit the true depth of his feelings. As another comrade, Angelica Balabanoff, described it, "I never saw such torment, I never saw any human being so completely absorbed by sorrow, by the effort to . . . guard it against the attention of others."

Lenin, however, had learned well

from his earlier experiences. In general, he knew how to keep his emotions "to himself," to "keep a stone in one's sling," and to regard all persons "without sentiment." It was because he had steeled himself to be "without sentiment" that he and the Bolshevik party he had formed around this ideal were able to rise to power when the times permitted it. Self-controlled, Lenin could control others; free of libidinal ties, Lenin could make a revolution without kid gloves.

At first glance, Gandhi might seem to be at the opposite pole from Lenin. Instead of hard, unsentimental relations, he preached love; instead of violent overthrow of the social system, he taught nonviolence; instead of a militant minority party, he sought an amorphous mass following. Indeed, there is some question whether Gandhi's efforts did, in fact, result in a revolution. I feel, however, that Gandhi *was* engaged in a revolution—a colonial revolution—and that closer examination shows him, as an ascetic revolutionary, to be similar to Lenin.

Gandhi's religious background was, of course, quite different from Lenin's. While some teachings of the Hindu sect in which Gandhi was raised, with its stress on cleanliness and purification, confession and vows, paralleled the teachings of Russian Orthodox Christianity, others, such as vegetarianism and ahimsa, or avoiding harm to living beings, were wholly absent from the Western religious tradition. In spite of these religious dissimilarities, the revolutionary traits of the two men were remarkably alike.

> "A man who is swayed by passions," Gandhi says,
>
> "may have good enough intentions,
>
> may be truthful in word, but he will never find the Truth.
>
> . . . A reformer cannot afford to have
>
> close intimacy with him whom he seeks to reform."

Gandhi, too, freed himself as much as possible from libidinal ties. His *Autobiography* is replete with testimonials to his efforts in this direction. "A man who is swayed by passions," he says, "may have good enough intentions, may be truthful in word, but he will never find the Truth [i.e., Satyagraha]." Again, he writes that "A reformer cannot afford to have close intimacy with him whom he seeks to reform. . . . I am of opinion that all exclusive intimacies are to be avoided . . . he who would be friends with God must remain alone or make the whole world his friend."

Gandhi equated the freeing of oneself from passion, from libidinal ties, with self-purification. Thus, he continues, "to attain to perfect purity one has to become absolutely passion-free in thought, speech and actions; to rise above the opposing currents of love and hatred, attachment and repulsion. I know that I have not in me as yet that triple purity, in spite of constant ceaseless striving for it. That is why the world's praise fails to move me, indeed it very often stings me. To conquer the subtle passions seems to me to be harder far than the physical conquest of the world by the force of arms."

Toward this end, Gandhi invoked the practice of self-control, of denial of impulse and desire, in short, of asceticism. Thus, when he went to London to study law, he vowed to abstain from meat, women, and wine. At thirty-six he embraced continence, swearing never again to have sexual relations, even with his own wife.

This self-control and denial of libidinal attachments would have remained only interesting character traits in a quaint little Indian lawyer had Gandhi not used them to free India from outside control. Erik Erikson, in his magnificent study *Gandhi's Truth,* argues persuasively that after long preparation and trials, and nearing the age of fifty, Gandhi stepped onto the stage of world history during a textile strike in Ahmedabad in 1918 by transmuting the ascetic practice of fasting into a political act. Gandhi himself wrote at the time: "I felt that it was a sacred moment for me, my faith was on the anvil, and I had no hesitation to rising and declaring to the men [on strike] that a breach of their vow so solemnly taken was unendurable by me and that I would not take any food until they had the 35 per cent increase given or until they had fallen. A meeting that was up to now unlike the former meetings, totally unresponsive, woke up as if by magic."

Fasting was a weapon—nonviolent, of course—to control primarily oneself and one's followers, and only secondarily one's opponents. Gandhi, unlike Lenin, aimed first at Truth and God. Only when these were attained, inside himself, could he have spiritual power over others.

Fasting was just one of Gandhi's spiritual weapons. Purification was another. And so was Gandhi's compulsion for self-cleanliness. This, too, he turned to political uses. At an annual meeting of the Indian Congress party, Gandhi writes in his *Autobiography,* "there was no limit to insanitation. Pools of water were everywhere. There were only a few latrines, and the recollection of their stink still oppresses me. I pointed it out to the volunteers. They said point-blank: 'That is not our work; it is the scavenger's work.' I asked for a broom. The men stared at me in wonder. I procured one and cleaned the latrine."

In this incident Gandhi's own compulsion is symbolically linked to the theme of "cleaning up" the corrupt political mess; it is tied to the destruction of caste lines, for scavenger's work was restricted to the untouchables; and it is connected to the modernizing of India, for cleanliness is essential to modern civilization.

This, then, can serve as a prototype for the way in which asceticism can be turned to revolutionary purposes. Gandhi's control over himself—his fasting, his denial of sexual impulses, his repression of libidinal attachments to people—gave him a spiritual power over his followers, and together they exerted a moral superiority over the British that eventually brought about freedom for India. This was Gandhi's revolution. Its nature is well summed up in the motto he offered his disciples: "Home Rule [Independence] equals Self Rule and Self Rule equals Self Control." Needless to say, operationally it was self-control that came first.

In both the West and in India there existed a religious tradition that supplied resonances to the revolutionary asceticism of a Lenin or a Gandhi. Such was not the case with Mao Tsetung in China. Yet he, too, exhibits many of the characteristic traits of the ascetic revolutionary. Indeed, it is in this light that the prototypal picture of the aged Mao swimming in the Yangtze River must be seen. Mao's swim helped symbolize his continued control

The image Mao presented

to his followers was that of a libidoless leader.

He taught the youth of China

that love . . . is a "psychosomatic activity which

consumes energy and wastes time."

over his mind and body, as well as over the river, and thus his right to rule the Chinese people.

As a boy Mao was caught up in an epic conflict with his father over the question of authority, and this personal struggle coincided with China's efforts to throw off the authority and control of the West. To accomplish this, China had to turn against its past and discard the authority and control of the Confucian system, and then reincarnate the old principles and values in a new form.

Mao exemplified this process in his personal life. When his father set him to studying the classics, he rebelled, turning instead to modern works; yet, once in power, he reasserted those same classical values in Communist garb. So, too, when his parents chose his wife for him in accordance with custom, Mao resisted, claiming free choice as the basis of all marriage; as chairman of the CCP, however, he insisted that free choice be sublimated to the dictates of the party, thereby putting himself in the place of a parent. "Mao Tse-tung is my father; the Communist party is my mother" was to be the refrain taught to small children in kindergarten.

I shall not go into the details of Mao's personal development here, but shall only single out a few instances relevant to our concern with revolutionary asceticism. The Yangtze River swim, for example, was based on Mao's youthful conversion to the very un-Chinese notion of physical education. He and his revolutionary companions, he says, "became ardent physical culturists." In his autobiography Mao describes their

regimen: "We slept in the open when frost was already falling and even in November swam in the cold rivers. . . . Perhaps it helped much to build the physique which I was to need so badly later on in my many marches back and forth across South China, and on the Long March from Kiangsi to the Northwest."

It was not only the body but the mind that was trained by Spartan living. In his 1917 article "A Study of Physical Culture," Mao explained that physical education was the necessary foundation for revolutionary regeneration. "Our nation is wanting in strength," he begins. The cultivation of physical and mental tranquillity, the contemplation advocated by Buddha and Lao-tse, is not the way to obtain it. Instead, "rude and savage exercise" is the path to strength, for exercise is the basis even of the intellectual knowledge that gives a man and a country power. "Physical education not only strengthens the body but also enhances our knowledge. . . . Physical strength is required to undertake the study of the numerous modern sciences, whether in school or through independent study. He who is equal to this is the man with a strong body."

The psychic significance of asceticism and displaced libido is strongly sounded in Mao's declaration that "we often observe that the weak are enslaved by their sentiments and are incapable of mastering them. Those whose senses are imperfect or whose limbs are defective are often enslaved by excessive passion, and reason is incapable of saving them. Hence it may be called an invariable law that when the body is

perfect and healthy, the sentiments are also correct . . . ." Thus, it was not just physique, honed by Spartan, ascetic training, that prepared Mao for the Long March and for guerrilla warfare in general; it was also the correct "sentiments," the control and mastery of passions.

Noteworthy, too, is Mao's stress on the dangers of "excessive passion," which he equates with enslavement. He and his comrades, he writes, were a "serious-minded little group of men and they had no time to discuss trivialities. Everything they did or said must have a purpose. They had no time for love or 'romance' and considered the times too critical and the need for knowledge too urgent to discuss women or personal matters. I was not interested in women. My parents had married me when I was fourteen to a girl of twenty, but I had never lived with her—and never subsequently did. I did not consider her my wife and at this time gave little thought to her."

When he was in his twenties, however, Mao did fall in love with a woman and marry her. But his wife, Yang K'ai-hui, was also a revolutionary, and an indication of how much time they might have had together can be gained from the numerous accounts of other such revolutionary marriages. Yang K'ai-hui was executed by the Kuomintang in 1930, and the fact that later in life Mao married an actress, Chiang Ch'ing, tells us almost nothing about his personal feelings.

Whatever the reality, the image Mao presented to his followers was that of a libidoless leader. In power, Mao taught the youth of China that love, as

It matters little that some of
the militant young have taken Mao Tse-tung as their hero.
We can see how much this is
play-acting if we recall that these militants frequently
embrace the drug scene, too.

a widely circulated official booklet puts it, is a "psychosomatic activity which consumes energy and wastes time." According to the magazine *Chinese Youth Fortnightly,* neither physical nor sentimental attractions are to play any part when marriage is contemplated. Instead, what counts is "a shared political consciousness which can lead to greater joint efforts in building Socialism and increasing production."

Rejection of the ties of love was directly connected to discipline. We see this clearly in the Red Army, in which the new man of China was first developed in numbers. In 1936 Edgar Snow called it "the only politically iron-clad army in China." The oblique allusion to Cromwell's Puritan army is borne out by the additional statement that "very few of the Reds smoked or drank: abstention was one of the 'eight disciplines' of the Red Army." (Mao, in fact, was an inveterate smoker, but he had to appear to share the self-discipline of his men.) Moreover, we are told, "the majority of the soldiers as well as officers of the Red Army were unmarried. Many of them were 'divorced'—that is, they had left their wives and families behind them."

It is, however, in thought reform that we see most clearly the exhortation to disregard personal feelings (or, at least, traditional feelings). Mao himself, in a speech of 1942, laid down the basic tenets: ". . . two principles must be observed. The first is 'punish the past to warn the future' and the second, 'save men by curing their ills.' Past error must be exposed *with no thought of personal feelings* [my italics] or face." By denying personal feelings, we can

"save" the man by converting him, just as Mao had earlier been converted to the true faith and behavior. Hardness, unsentimentality, lack of feeling—these were Mao's injunctions to his followers. Well might he have said what his youthful Red Guards are reputed to have said: "Demolition bombs and hand grenades will be thrown . . . Let what is called 'human affection' . . . get out of the way."

Mao, then, like Lenin and Gandhi, cultivated the traits of the ascetic revolutionary. Perhaps because of the effective absence of an ascetic tradition in Chinese culture, it seems to have been political need rather than personal pressure that caused him to curtail his libidinal impulses. Whatever the reason, Mao's success as a revolutionary was to a significant extent based on the fact that he was, or appeared to be, an ascetic revolutionary.

Will an ascetic-revolutionary leader, such as a Lenin, Gandhi, or Mao, appear on the American scene? The answer, of course, will largely depend on whether a truly revolutionary political situation emerges in the United States. For the moment, one does not exist. It matters little that some of the militant young have taken Mao Tse-tung as their hero. We can see how much this is play-acting if we recall that these militants frequently embrace the drug scene, too. In China, of course, Mao has forbidden the consumption of opium as debilitating and antirevolutionary. What I am suggesting here is that self-indulgent people rarely possess the character traits necessary to become professional revolutionaries. So, too,

the youthful cry "Make love, not war": while it is highly appealing to nonrevolutionary ears, it is hardly the right spiritual preparation for a revolution without kid gloves.

At the moment, there are few signs of the emergence of the ascetic-revolutionary type. But the increasing attempts of federal and local authorities to crack down on revolutionary aesthetes—in reaction to the confrontation tactics of the young, which are still in the realm of play-acting—may bring about the kinds of conditions that make ascetic revolutionaries. Some of these "victims" of repression may well become professional revolutionaries. Once jailed, they may see little possibility of a successful career in the Establishment, even if they did wish to return to it. Once beaten up, their anger may congeal into a total hatred of the system that they think stands behind the police force.

If, for these reasons and others, they turn to revolution as their professional activity, I believe we shall see an exchange of aestheticism for asceticism. The new motto is more likely to be "Make revolution, not love." When this happens, and ascetic-revolutionary types are conspicuously present, we shall know that a truly revolutionary situation (though one that offers, I suspect, few potentialities for success) is upon us.

With Erik Erikson and others, Bruce Mazlish is keenly interested in the psychological approach to history, a field in which he has done notable work. An article by him on James and John Stuart Mill appeared in the Summer, 1970, HORIZON.

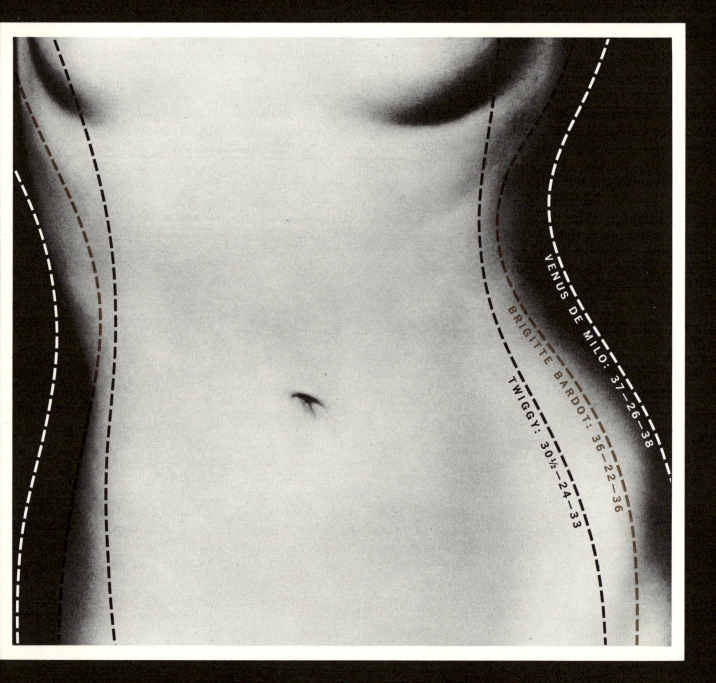

VENUS DE MILO: 37—26—38

BRIGITTE BARDOT: 36—22—36

TWIGGY: 30½—24—33

No shoe is too bone-breaking

nor corset too breathtaking nor bodily alteration

too excruciating

for man not to have tried it out in his

continuing pursuit of

The Fashionable Body

The urge to alter his body is felt by man only; animals, enjoying the advantage of healthier instincts, do not share it. Although the human shape was designed by the greatest of artists, His taste does not necessarily coincide with ours; at no time did man accept the image in which he was created as final. He decided early that there was room for improvement.

Neither prehistoric cave dweller nor late-industrial urban man considered the human body aesthetically satisfactory. The Aurignacians and Magdalenians practiced mutilation of their hands with the same confidence that modern man brings to crippling his feet. Uneducated and oversophisticated alike seem to act on an uncontrollable impulse to rearrange their anatomy; no part of the body is spared from more or less violent interference.

Whatever man's reasons for wanting to change his physique, whatever the relevance of his narcissistic or autoerotic inclinations, the factor that goes farthest to account for this unholy obsession is boredom. Bored with the natural shape of his body, he delights in getting away from himself, and to judge from past and present performances, the resources at hand for making his escape are inexhaustible. Only rarely does he exercise self-restraint. To the ancient Greeks, for instance, the human body was inviolate, or almost: some plucked their pubic hair.

In the beginning, man himself was clay and canvas. Body painting and body sculpture were fused into a single production and thus accounted for a harmonious work of art. Indeed, we should not hesitate to regard them as the oldest form of art. At any rate, the use of the body as the artist's medium rather than his inspiration antedates the more conventional categories of plastic art.

Works of art often exist only in the minds of those who create them, and the so-called improvements perpetrated on our anatomy are no exception. "It is certainly not true," observed Charles Darwin, "that there is in the mind of man any universal standard of beauty with respect to the human body. It is, however, possible that certain tastes may in the course of time become inherited . . ." Without going into the deeper motives of why certain human forms give us pleasure and others do not, Darwin scoffed at Western man's conceits. "If all our women," he argued, "were to become as beautiful as the Venus de' Medici, we should for a time be charmed; but we should soon wish for variety; and as soon as we had obtained variety, we should wish to see certain characters a little exaggerated beyond the then existing common standard." As we shall see, a little exaggeration goes a long way.

It is, of course, doubtful that a modern woman blessed with the proportions of a Greek statue would be happy. Broad hips have not been fashionable for a long time, and what modern shoe could accommodate a classical foot? But then, even in Darwin's time, the shape of the Medicean Venus (a mere copy of a Greek sculpture) was thought to be on the dowdy side. Changeable ideals of beauty have always been far more desirable than everlasting perfection, and with good reason.

Our laws permit a man to have as many wives as he pleases, provided he marries them successively. Since, however, this staggered sort of polygamy is often beyond a man's means, the way to make the monotony of marital life tolerable is to split a wife's personality. But masquerading alone won't do the trick. A new dress or a sun tan does not turn her into a new woman; the change has to be more than skin deep. Let us examine some of the alterations that she—or he—has accomplished in the pursuit of physical variety. —B.R.

On the figure opposite, which represents the currently fashionable and supposedly (sigh!) average female torso, are sketched the contours of three disparate forms: that of Twiggy, of Brigitte Bardot, and of a robust lady called Venus de Milo. In body styles as well as in ethics, apparently, the function of the constantly changing ideal is to make it ever more difficult to remain cheerfully average.

By BERNARD RUDOFSKY

One of the boldest ways to interfere with human anatomy is to mold the skull. Among tribes who practice this art, it is part and parcel of a child's upbringing. It calls for special skills and has traditionally been a mother's duty and, we may presume, pleasure. The first provocation for a mother's pinching and kneading her baby's skull was perhaps its yielding softness. Playful handling developed into more conscious efforts to deform, and racial and aesthetic concepts were added later. Thus, broad heads were broadened, flat noses flattened closer to the face, a tapering occiput sharpened to a point—a shape mostly associated today with humanoids from outer space. These spectacular forms were

Steatopygous Bushwoman

achieved with the aid of contraptions no more ingenious than a common mousetrap.

Admiration for elongated heads has been widespread among such dissimilar peoples as the ancient Egyptians, the American Indians, and the provincial French. In some parts of France the custom of binding a child's head was observed as late as the last century. Contrary to what one would expect from a nation known for setting ideals of elegance for much of the world, the motives for this kind of head deformation were eugenic rather than aesthetic. People believed that a child's vocation could be guided, literally, by shaping his brain. One nineteenth-century Jesuit priest, a Father Josset, advised mothers to work on the heads of their newborn children so that they might one day become great orators.

It was a time when phrenology was the last word in head control. Purportedly a science, phrenology dealt with the conformation of the skull. The shape of a person's head was supposed to determine his aptitudes and his moral character, and it was thought that a direct relationship existed between the faculties of the mind and the separate portions of the brain, each portion representing a distinct mental or moral disposition. The number of faculties varied from twenty-seven to thirty-five, depending on the phrenologist's persuasion. They were classified in categories that strike us today as rather whimsical: Religion; Wit; Ideality; Cunning; Marvellousness; Mimicry; Murder; Wonder; and so forth.

Persons who had their heads examined late in life often realized with dismay that they had missed a chance of being massaged into a genius. Eventually, the "art of reading bumps," as it was called in the United States, became so successful that an American university established a professorship of phrenology. Observed the *Encyclopedia Americana:* "The most necessary thing for a professor of phrenology was a happy faculty of flattering everybody." Alas, not only art but science as well is subject to the fashions of the day. Thus, phrenology has given way to aptitude tests, while squeezing heads has been abandoned in favor of squeezing toes.

Another, far more enduring, not to say endearing, sort of body deformation is obesity. Admired in many parts of the world, obesity has rated—as far

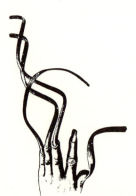

Chinese tendril talons

MUSÉE DE L'HOMME, PARIS

Elongated Congolese head

as women are concerned —as a secondary sexual characteristic. To judge from prehistoric art, fat women either predominated or were used by choice as artists' models, and in the course of time the well-upholstered woman was favored over the scrawny one. A similar taste can frequently be found in modern art; the artist who does not limit his sympathies to the fashionably disembodied female sides with the primitive and celebrates massive womanhood.

Since only women of leisure can afford the luxury of being immobilized, the languid and overfed woman came to represent the well-to-do and beautiful; obesity became a mark of quality. Among those primitives who gauge female beauty by sheer bulk, brides-to-be go through preparations of excessive fattening. On reaching puberty, a girl is placed in a special fattening-hut. The time of seclusion varies from six months to two years, depending on the wealth of her parents.

Some tribes discriminate in their admiration for obesity between overall bulk and specific, strategically placed cushions of fat. The most celebrated among salient features is steatopygia, the overdevelopment of the subcutaneous fat that covers a woman's hind parts and upper thighs. Unlike the judges of our beauty contests, who have their eyes on a prominently cantilevered bosom, buttock lovers, according to Darwin, would make their selection by "ranging [their women] in a line, and by picking her out who projects farthest *a tergo.*"

Western woman, whom nature forgot to endow with a magnificent rear end, at times had to rely on make-believe to render herself desirable; witness the bustle of the 1870's, a gross illusion of steatopygia. Subsequently, man's admiration shifted to the stout woman with a tiny waist, a combination that does not occur in nature. It cannot be produced by crossbreeding

LEFT: COLLECTION OF BERNARD RUDOFSKY; FAR LEFT: MUSEUM OF NATURAL HISTORY, LONDON

or special exercise; it exists only as a sartorial illusion, achieved by applying a vise known as a corset.

In approaching this subject we have to keep in mind that the woman who lived at the turn of the century barely resembled today's woman. She had missed an important phase in the evolution of mankind, for she could not stand straight unaided. To ensure her upright position she needed support, and it was the corset that saved her from having to walk on all fours.

Precautions against her breakdown had to be taken early in life. The little girl was securely encased in a junior corset that promised Perfect Health and visibly improved the contours of her shrimplike body. To be sure, the use of a child's corset was not limited to Occidental countries. Circassian girls—to give but one foreign example —wore from the tenth year on a broad girdle of untanned leather. The wealthy locked it with silver hooks, whereas common people sewed it tightly around

Chad castanets

the waist. One writer, familiar with Circassian lore, tells us that mothers fastened their daughters "into saffian leather garments for seven years to give their figures greater symmetry." This cuirass was worn until the wedding night, "when the bridegroom with a sharp-cutting dagger unties the Gordian knot, which ceremony is frequently attended with danger."

The corset of our grandmothers was a masterpiece of functional design. It operated on three levels—mechanical, aesthetic, and moral. "The corset," wrote Thorstein Veblen, the foremost portraitist of the leisure class, "is, in

The rotund rump: removable and permanent

economic theory, substantially a mutilation, undergone for the purpose of lowering the subject's vitality and rendering her permanently and obviously unfit for work. It is true, the corset impairs the personal attraction of the wearer [Veblen refers of course to the naked woman], but the loss suffered on that score is offset by the gain in reputability which comes of her visibly increased expensiveness and infirmity." The natural outline of the female waist, unredeemed by art, was not savory enough for man. It was the *corsetière's* business to attack the aesthetic problem at its roots by bending women's bones into an alluring shape.

The whalebone corset marked an advanced technique of disfigurement. Although this mechanism, with its stays and ribbons, was a comedown from the all-metal corset, the results were complex enough. Not only did the corset claw into the flesh, it played havoc with the inner organs by displacing them, eventually leading to a number of ailments. Occasionally, it caused miscarriages. On the credit side was the heightened seductiveness of the wearer, her embraceability, so to speak: the pressure applied to the waist produced the desired simultaneous inflation of the chest and buttocks, and the latter could be still further accentuated by the bustle.

The corset's crippling effects on the female body were persistently ignored, much as today we ignore the consequences of wearing deforming shoes. The would-be guardian of our health, the phy-

sician, whose business it is to keep us in good working order, was as reluctant to interfere with fashion's dictum then as he is today. His warnings were sounded timidly, or at any rate ineffectively. He plied his trade oblivious of, or in tacit agreement with, the abuses of the day. As a man he was not immune to the corset's fascination; as a doctor he hesitated to condemn the corset for fear of being considered immoral. Respectful of manufacturers and their products, he did not permit himself much criticism. Occasionally,

Embossed Congolese flesh

he was even known to pimp for them or, better, turn predatory and go into business himself.

To give an example, in the 1880's a Dr. Scott put on the market an unbreakable electric corset, guaranteed to cure quickly paralysis and rheumatism, spinal complaints, dyspepsia, constipation, impaired circulation, liver and kidney troubles, nervous debility, numbness, and so forth. "Constructed on scientific principles," the advertisement assured the gullible woman, "their therapeutic value is unquestioned." When worn constantly, even "nightly, too, if desired," the corset also imparted to one's system "the required amount of *odic force* which Nature's law demands."

Odic force, a now-forgotten nineteenth-century discovery, was then much on people's minds, thanks to the persuasive power of advertising. Od was a gift of nature, like perfect pitch. Those who had it were endowed with excruciating sensibility. They could di-

Flattening a Chinook's head

59

vine a vein of ore in a mountain, or, more spectacularly, start a pendulum swinging without touching it. Those whom nature had neglected could, if they wished, have recourse to odic contraptions such as Dr. Scott's corset, whose miraculous powers were attested to, believe it or not, by a surgeon general of the United States. Eventually, the scientific theory collapsed and od became odious.

Everything considered, doctors' knowledge of the female anatomy was less than perfect mainly because they based their observations on the deformed body. They were misled about such elementary performances as breathing; not only woman's skeleton but also her breathing apparatus was thought to function differently from man's. "Until recent years," wrote Havelock Ellis in 1910, "it was commonly supposed that there is a real and fundamental difference in breathing between men and women, that women's breathing is thoracic and men's abdominal. It is now known that under natural and healthy conditions there is no difference, but that men and women breathe in a precisely identical manner." If doctors had wanted to, they could easily have found "natural and healthy conditions" among noncorset-wearing women the world over.

Withal, corset manufacturers did not overlook the male body as potential modeling clay in their hands. Although the wearing of a corset was mainly a woman's prerogative (and duty), the fops and drones among men were not long in adopting it. "The corset mania,"

Mom and molded moppet, 1886

we read in the Springfield *Republican* of 1903, "began with the military men —they compare notes on corsets- in some of the army clubs as gravely as they discuss the education bill at the National Library Club." In all fairness we must grant them in retrospect their inalienable right to body deformation. They were not the first to squeeze their waists; wasp waists were common as far back as archaic Greece. The last holdout for male waist constriction is Papua, provided the old customs are still honored.

At a distance of more than three generations, our great-grandmothers' fanatic loyalty to the wasp-waist ideal would seem absurd were it not that we now understand its deeper significance much better. Far more than a crutch, the corset was a hallmark of virtue. The belief that clothes are designed in good measure to punish the flesh never really lost its hold on us; in a way we are still doing penance for Adam's sin. Though clothes may not always be the best protection against nature's rigors, they often represent instruments of moral philosophy. The attraction of the agreeably punitive hair shirt has not worn off; metamorphosed variously into garter, girdle, waistband, and brassière, it has played on some of the focal points of the body, leaving an imprint. Bruises have often been accepted as the inevitable consequences of wearing clothes. Perhaps there lingers in women's minds the consoling thought that *their* mothers endured far greater inconvenience.

When the harm that resulted from

wearing a corset was belatedly recognized—and cavalierly dismissed—the fashion that lent an edge to men's inexhaustible appetite for swooning females was vindicated on moral grounds. People who lived in what was, from the point of view of costume history, a crustaceous age, thought of the whalebone corset as a kind of Jeanne d'Arc armor. Uncorseted women reeked of license; an unlaced waist was regarded as a vessel of sin. A heretic like Isadora Duncan, heralded by Rodin and other connoisseurs of the human physique as the embodiment of Greece, helped only to further strengthen the popular belief that the lack of a corset (or shoes) was a visible sign of depravity. Indeed, some

Bunny in a cinch

men associate women's gradual liberation from the girdle and the garter as just another sympton of the immorality of our age.

Every generation has its own demented ideas on supporting some part of the human anatomy. Older people still remember a time when everybody went through life ankle-supported. Young and old wore laced boots. A shoe that did not reach well above the ankle was considered disastrous to health. What, one asks, has become of ankle support, once so warmly recommended by doctors and shoe salesmen? What keeps our ankles from breaking down these days of low-cut shoes?

Ankle support has given way to arch support; millions of shoe-buying people are determined to "preserve their

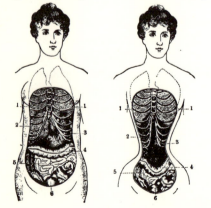

Organ-grinding: health vs. the corset, 1904

The hourglass figure achieved: in having a rib removed, actress Anna Held pinched herself to death.

OPPOSITE: BROWN BROTHERS; THIS PAGE, LEFT-HAND COLUMN: COLLECTION OF BERNARD RUDOFSKY; MIDDLE COLUMN: *Harper's Bazaar*, 1886

COURTESY OF THE PLAYBOY CLUB, NEW YORK

metatarsal arch" without so much as suspecting that it does not exist. Nevertheless, the fiction of the arch is being perpetuated to help sell "supports" and "preservers" on an impressive scale.

The dread of fallen arches is, however, a picayune affair compared to that other calamity, the foot's asymmetry. I am not talking about the difference within a single pair of feet, that is, the difference between the right and left foot of a person; I mean the asymmetry of the foot itself.

Few of us are truly aware that an undeformed foot's outline is *not* symmetrical. It is distinctly lopsided. Let us take a close look at it: the big toe

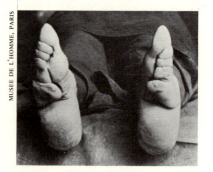

A Chinese woman's dainty bound feet

extends from one to two inches beyond the fifth toe. More important, the five toes spread out fanlike. They do not converge to a point in front as one would expect from the shape of the shoe. Quite the contrary, they converge to a point in back of the heel. It should be obvious, even to the least observant person, that to conform to the outline of a shoe, the big toe ought to be in the place of the third one, that is, in the center.

Shoe manufacturers have shown admirable patience with nature. Despite or because of the absence of feet that live up to their commercial ideals of anatomy, they doggedly go on producing symmetrical shoes. And although their customers' feet have not changed in the course of time, they spare no effort or expense to come up every season with a new (symmetrical) shoe for the same old foot. (The pathological hate of the natural form of the foot is no-

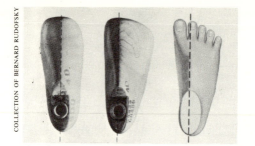

Real and ideal: baby lasts versus baby foot

where more forcibly expressed than in the commandments of the Shakers, which say that "it is contrary to order to have right and left shoes.")

By some atavistic quirk of nature, every normal baby is born with undeformed feet. The forepart of the foot—measured across the toes—is about twice as wide as the heel. The toes barely touch each other and are as nimble as fingers. Were the child able to keep up his toe twiddling, he might easily retain as much control over his feet as over his hands. Not that we see anything particularly admirable in nimble toes; they strike us as freakish, perhaps since we associate prehensile feet with primitive civilizations. To our twisted mind, the foot in its undamaged state is anachronistic, if not altogether barbaric. Ever since the shoe became the badge of admission to Western civilization—in rural countries such as Portugal and Brazil the government exhorts peasants to wear shoes in the name of progress—we have looked down on barefooted or sandaled nations.

Since wearing shoes is synonymous with wearing *bad* shoes, the modern shoe inevitably becomes an instrument of deformation. The very concept of the modern shoe does not admit of an intelligent solution; it is not made to fit a human foot but to fit a wooden last whose shape is determined by the whim of the designer. Whereas a tailor allows for a customer's unequal shoulders and arms, and an optometrist prescribes different lenses for the right and left eye, we buy shoes of identical size and dimensions for our right and left foot, conveniently forgetting—or ignoring—that, as a rule, they are not of the same width and length. Even in countries where it is still possible to

find an artisan who is willing to make a pair of shoes to order, chances are that he works on mass-produced lasts and comes up with a product that, shapewise, is not much different from the industrial one.

In both the manufacturer's and the customer's opinion the shoe comes before the foot. It is less intended to protect the foot from cold and dirt than to mold it into a fashionable shape. Most infants' shoes are liable to dislocate the bones and bend the foot into the shoe shape. The child does not mind the interference; "never expect the child to complain that the shoe is hurting him," says the podiatrist Dr. Simon Wikler, "for the crippling process is painless." According to a ten-year study of the Podiatry Society of the state of New York, 99 per cent of all feet are perfect at birth, 8 per cent have developed troubles at one year, 41 per cent at the age of five, and 80 per cent at twenty. "We limp into adulthood," the report concludes.

"Medical Schools," another doctor says, "fail almost completely in giving the student a sound grounding and a sane therapeutic concept of foot conditions." And in *Military Medicine* one reads that "there has been no objective test that could be readily incorporated in physical examinations, or taught to medical students, pediatricians, or physicians in military and industrial medicine, that would enable them to recognize deformities of the foot . . ."

To top it all, modern man, perhaps unknown to himself, is afflicted with a diffuse shoe-fetishism. Inherited prejudices derived from the Cinderella complex, practices whose origins and reasons escape him, and traditional obtuseness combine to make him tol-

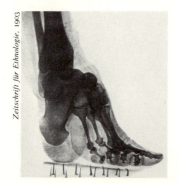

X ray of a bound foot

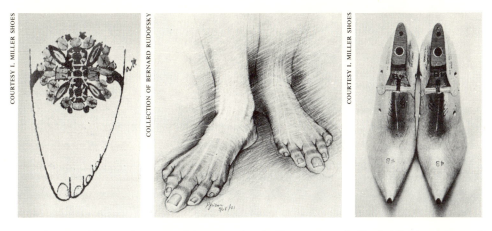

Feet that would fit a modern pointed shoe were sketched by artists Andy Warhol (left) and Bernard Pfriem (center). Genetic engineers or shoe manufacturers—who will have the last laugh (right)?

erate the deformities inflicted by his shoes. In this respect his callousness matches that of the Chinese of old. In fact, if he ever felt a need to justify the shoes' encroachments on his anatomy, he could cite bound feet (if he had ever heard of them), the Chinese variety of the "correctly shaped" foot.

Recent version of a "bound" foot

This exotic custom, which lasted nearly one thousand years, did not extend over the whole country; the Manchus, including the imperial family, never practiced foot-binding. Small feet are a racial characteristic of Chinese women, and the desire to still further reduce their size in the name of beauty seems to have been strong enough to make women tolerate irrevocable mutilation. As so often happens, people derive infinitely greater satisfaction from an artifact, however crude, than from nature's product. Besides, not only were a woman's stunted feet highly charged with erotic symbolism, they made her eligible for

marriage. Without them she was reduced to spinsterhood. Her desirability as a love object was in direct proportion to her inability to walk. It ought to be easy for our women to understand the mentality of the Chinese men; every woman knows that to wear "walking shoes"—as derogatory a term as "sensible shoes"—puts a damper on a man's ardor. The effect of absurdly impractical shoes, on the other hand, is as intoxicating as a love potion. The girl child who puts on a pair of high-heeled shoes is magically propelled into womanhood.

Modern woman is not averse to maltreating her feet for reasons similar to those of her ancient Chinese sisters, and therefore will make allowances for bunions, calluses, corns, ingrown toenails, and hammer toes. But she draws the line at a major interference with her foot skeleton. Unwilling to bother with growing her own organic high heels, she has to get along with artificial ones.

As costume props go, high heels have a relatively short history. In the middle of the seventeenth century this new device for corrupting the human walk was added to the footwear of the elegant, putting them, as it were, on tiptoe. The ground, indoors and outdoors, came to a tilt, so to speak, and for fashion's sake, people began to walk on a portable incline. As the ordinary folk continued to wear flat-bottomed shoes, heeled footwear, com-

bined with a strutting walk, became a mark of distinction.

But the times were anything but favorable to the new invention. On the street the well-heeled had to avail themselves of a sedan chair to avoid the cobblestones underfoot, while indoors they found it difficult to negotiate the polished parquet and marble floors that were the pride of the epoch. And yet, men took to high heels as enthusiastically as women did. To judge from paintings of the time, fashionable men could not have cared less for "walking shoes."

Did men's high-heeled shoes and fine stockings turn a woman's head? Were women smitten by the sight of a man's well-turned ankle and slender leg? For whereas their own legs remained hidden by crinolines, men proudly displayed their calves and gave as much attention to them as to their wigs. Silicone injections still being centuries away, a skinny fellow made up for any natural deficiency by padding. Eventually, the French Revolution brought men and women down to earth. Dandies and *élégantes* wore paper-thin flat soles without, it seems,

Defying fashion: foot-fitting shoe

depriving themselves of their mutual attraction. Years later, when high heels reappeared on the fashionable scene, they were relegated to woman's domain; so far, men have not left the ground again.

In lucid moments we look with amazement at the fraud we perpetrate on ourselves—the bruises, mutilations, and dislocated bones—but if we feel at all uncomfortable, it is not for long. An automatic self-defense mechanism blurs our judgment and makes right and wrong exchange places. Moreover, some violations of the body are sanctioned by religion, while others are simply the price of a man's admittance to his tribe, regardless of whether he lives in the bush or in a modern metropolis. The sense of superiority he derives from, say, circumcision is no less real than that of the owner of a pair of bound feet. Physicians have always been of two minds about it; "to cut off the top of the uppermost skin of the secret parts," maintained Dr. John Bulwer in *Anthropometamorphosis* (1653) "is directly against the honesty of Nature, and an injurious unsufferable trick put upon her." And a contemporary pediatrician, E. Noel Preston, writing in the *Journal of the American Medical Association*, considers circumcision "little better than mutilation." The very real dangers of the operation, such as infection and hemorrhage, outweigh the fancied advantages of cancer prevention. "If a child can be taught to tie his shoes or brush his teeth or wash behind the ears," says Dr. Preston, "he can also be taught to wash beneath his foreskin."

A change of allegiance may lead to double mutilation, as in the paradoxical phenomenon of uncircumcision: after the subjugation of Palestine by Alexander the Great, those Jews who found it desirable to turn into Gentiles underwent a painful operation that restored to them the missing prepuce.

Sometimes such mutilation reaches a high degree of ferocity. Among some Arab tribes circumcision is performed as an endurance test for youths who have come of age. "It consists," writes the Hebrew scholar Raphael Patai, "in the cutting of the skin across the stomach below the navel and thence down to the thighs, after which it is peeled off, leaving the stomach, the pelvis, the penis, the scrotum, and the inner legs uncovered and flayed. Many young men are said to have succumbed to the ordeal which in recent years has been prohibited by

Silicone: mammary improver

the Saudi Arabian government." However, the custom has not disappeared, doubtless because of its sex appeal. The ceremony takes place in female company—that is, in the presence of the young men's brides-to-be, who may refuse to marry their intended if they betray their agony by so much as a hint of discomfort.

Man's obsession with violating his body is not just of anthropological interest; it also helps us to understand the irrationality of dress. The devices for interfering with human anatomy are paralleled by a host of contraptions that simulate deformation or are simply meant to cheat the eye: bustles, pads, heels, wedges, codpieces, brassières, and so forth. Once, thirty years marked the end of a woman's desirability. In time, this age limit was gradually ex-

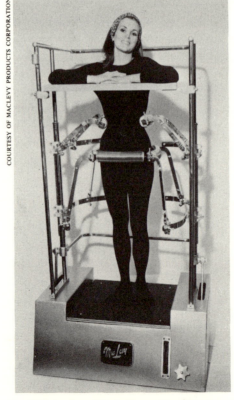

COURTESY OF MACLEVY PRODUCTS CORPORATION

Waist not, want not: Space Age slimming

The women opposite, exercising in a New York gym in 1910, have rejected the corset but not the dream of the fashionable body.

tended and pushed to a point where it got lost altogether. In order not only to look eternally young but also fashionable, she had to obey ever-changing body ideals.

Thus a woman born at the turn of the century was a buxom maiden in accordance with the dictates of the day. Photographs testify to the generosity of her charms, although her tender age ought to raise doubts about their authenticity. In the 1920's, when maturity and motherhood had come to her, pictures record an angular, lean, flatchested creature. Since she did not want to renounce her attractiveness, she had to submit to an extremely unfeminine beauty ideal. Twenty years later, she was rotund again and commanded the undiminished attention of the other sex. Today, she is still in the running, ever ready to overhaul her body to prolong her youth beyond biological limits. She has inflamed three generations of men, each loyal to a different image of perfection.

Alas, an aged body, however arresting and deceptive the results of its updating and remodeling may be, imparts to its owner only a limited sense of youth. It serves mainly as a stylish peg for clothes. In other words, it is the clothed body that triumphs, not the naked one. As Herbert Spencer said: "The consciousness of being perfectly dressed may bestow a peace such as religion cannot give."

Bernard Rudofsky is known for his unorthodox opinions about the various comforts (more often discomforts) man has devised for himself—architectural, culinary, and sartorial. He has written for HORIZON *about stairs, cave dwellings, streets, and most recently (Spring, 1971), castles. This article is taken from his book* The Unfashionable Human Body, *to be published by Doubleday in October. It is a revision of his classic* Are Clothes Modern?, *published in 1947.*

THE SHADOW OF
THE
OLMECS

Who were these mysterious forerunners of the Mayas and the Aztecs?

More than one hundred years ago, in 1862, a Mexican scholar named José Maria Melgar set out from a sugar-cane hacienda on the lower slopes of the Tuxtla Mountains, in southern Veracruz, Mexico, to look into a report of a gigantic inverted "kettle" the natives had discovered buried in the soil. Instead of the "kettle," he found a ten-ton

This statue of a ball player, with ratcheted sockets for movable arms, was deliberately decapitated.

basalt head, the "Ethiopic" features of which led him to believe that African Negroes had settled here in remote antiquity. His subsequent article describing this stone, one of a dozen such "Colossal Heads" now known, was the first published account of an object typical of what is called the Olmec civilization.

Just who were the Olmecs?

They were the first American Indians to achieve a level of social, cultural, and artistic complexity high enough for them to be called civilized. As such, they were precursors of

A laborer on the author's 1966 expedition poses with a five-and-one-half-ton Colossal Head found in the Mexican jungle. Carved from basalt by sculptors who had no metal tools, it may be a portrait of an Olmec king.

the later Mexican and Central American cultures, whose great achievements could not have been realized without them.

Though we are familiar with the Aztec empire, and know something of the Mayas, the name "Olmec" probably means little to most of us. Yet today Olmec archaeology is laying bare one of the most exciting chapters in the history of our continent. Imagine a people capable of carving human heads on a gigantic scale and exquisite figurines from blue-green, translucent jade. Imagine an art style based on the combined features of a snarling jaguar and a human infant. Then transport these people back beyond all known Indian civilizations, to a distance in time of more than three thousand years, and put them down in the inhospitable, swampy jungles of Mexico's Gulf Coast.

The extraordinary discovery Melgar made in these jungles went largely unnoticed until the first decade of this century, when the stone was visited by the German scholar Eduard Seler. Then it was again forgotten by the archaeological world. Forgotten, that is, until the 1920's, when the pioneer archaeologists Frans Blom and Oliver La Farge discovered the great, swamp-bound site of La Venta. There they found another Colossal Head, along with a number of other great stone sculptures in a style they mistakenly ascribed to the Mayas.

La Venta intrigued several other scholars, who quickly noted that this style, while highly sophisticated, was very different from that of the Classic Mayas, who flourished in the Yucatán Peninsula and farther south from about A.D. 300 to 900. They also noticed that some figurines and ceremonial axes of jade and other fine stones that had been turning up in museums and private collections were stylistically similar to the objects found at La Venta. They christened the unknown, non-Mayan civilization that had produced them "Olmec," after the mysterious tribe (whose name meant "Rubber People" in the Aztec tongue) that dominated the southern Gulf Coast of Mexico on the eve of the Spanish Conquest. But who were the *archaeological* Olmecs? How old was their civilization, and what was its relationship to the other civilizations of Mexico and Central America, for example, the Mayan or Toltec? Only in recent years has enough attention been paid to these questions to provide at least partial answers.

The foundations of scientific archaeology in the Olmec area were laid by Matthew W. Stirling of the Smithsonian Institution during his expeditions between 1938 and 1946. The first task Stirling set for himself was that of excavating Tres Zapotes, the site of Melgar's Ethiopic head. There he came upon an Olmec-type carved stone, the now-famous Stela C, which bore a date in the Mayan system that seemed to match a day in the year 31 B.C.—over three centuries earlier than the most ancient date then known for the Mayas.

This and other leads suggested to Stirling, as it did to leading Mexican archaeologists, that the Olmec civilization was probably the most ancient high culture yet known for the New World. After 1940 Stirling moved to La Venta, in neighboring Tabasco, and continued to make spectacular Olmec discoveries, particularly tombs of extraordinary richness.

One group, however, remained skeptical; the Mayan specialists. It seemed heresy to these American and British archaeologists to believe that the upstart Olmec civilization could have predated—and according to Stirling and his Mexican colleagues, even foreshadowed—Classic Mayan culture, which in many respects represented the highest achievement of the American Indian. Since 1840 the world had known and appreciated the splendid achievements of the ancient Mayas in writing, astronomy, calendrical science, art, and architecture. It was inconceivable that the Olmecs could have flourished before A.D. 300. Few Mayan buffs were ready to admit that Stela C at Tres Zapotes was a date to be read in the Mayan system.

The controversy over the Olmecs could not be settled until the advent of radiocarbon dating. In 1955 a University of California team under Dr. Robert F. Heizer opened a series of trenches at La Venta and secured a

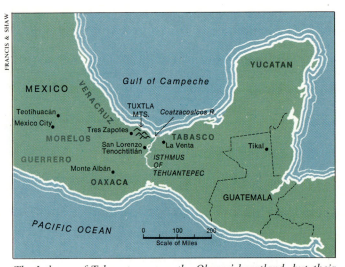

FRANCIS & SHAW

The Isthmus of Tehuantepec was the Olmecs' heartland, but their influence spread west into Mexico and south into Central America.

large number of charcoal samples. Most of the radiocarbon dates turned out to be far older than anyone would then have thought possible: 800–400 B.C. Incredibly, Olmec culture seems to have been at its height *seven to eleven* centuries before that of the Classic Mayas. La Venta—with its gigantic basalt monuments, mosaic pavements of serpentine blocks, a hundred-foot-high earthen pyramid, caches of carved jade and serpentine, and other wonders—was not a town or city in the usual sense but a mysteriously remote center for ceremonies and politics, isolated on its swamp-bound island. Why did it exist at all? And where did its builders come from?

There was no easy answer to the second question. Olmec sculptures had been found along the Gulf Coast as far north as the city of Veracruz, Olmec reliefs carved on a cliff had been located in the state of Morelos, and Olmec jades had turned up in puzzling profusion in the western state of Guerrero. The frequency of such finds prompted Miguel Covarrubias, the talented artist-archaeologist and long-time proponent of Olmec antiquity, to suggest Guerrero as the Olmec homeland, on the theory that they must have learned to carve small figures before moving to Veracruz and Tabasco, where their gigantic monuments are concentrated.

But many archaeologists, including myself, were convinced that Olmec origins would some day be found in the Olmec "heartland," the crescent-shaped, low-lying region along the Gulf Coast. Since the highest development of the culture was surely there, then why couldn't its beginnings, perhaps as far back in the pre-Classic period as 1500 B.C., also be there?

My own quest for Olmec origins—and for the conditions, ecological or otherwise, that may have stimulated the rise of native American civilization—led me, in December, 1964, on a trip of exploration up the sluggish, meandering Coatzacoalcos River, which drains the northern part of the Isthmus of Tehuantepec, to a riverside village called Tenochtitlán. A few miles south of the village lies a jungle-covered mesa known as San Lorenzo. In 1945 Matthew Stirling had been taken there by local Indians who had seen a great stone eye staring up from the dirt of a trail crossing the mesa. The eye turned out to belong to a new Colossal Head, one of a number of basalt monuments that Stirling found and excavated that season and the next. Some of these multi-ton heads, with their "football" helmets, flat faces, and staring eyes, have traveled as far afield as Leningrad and are the best-known examples of Olmec achievement in sculpture.

Two mysteries had immediately presented themselves to Stirling at San Lorenzo. First, the basalt from which the heads and other stones were carved did not occur anywhere around the site, the nearest source lying some fifty miles to the northwest.

The second mystery concerned the final disposition of the sculptures. Almost all of them were found either lying on the bottoms or the slopes of the deep, jungle-filled ravines that cut into the San Lorenzo mesa. Stirling guessed that some non-Olmec invaders had smashed or otherwise mutilated the monuments and then pushed them into the ravines. If so, there would be little chance of dating the Olmec occupation of San Lorenzo by associating the sculptures with archaeological layers.

The idea of mounting a major archaelogical effort at San Lorenzo came to me during my trip in 1964. By the end of the next year I found myself, aluminum camera case in perspiring hand, standing in the grass-covered "street" of Tenochtitlán looking in vain for a sympathetic face. The natives were decidedly *not* friendly. Those Colossal Heads that had gone around

the world had been removed by Veracruz archaeologists without the villagers' approval, and they were angry. Even so, I felt sure that a little diplomacy would make it possible to work there, and my optimism proved to be justified. We eventually claimed the majority of the local villagers as our friends and colleagues.

In 1966 Yale University, with financial backing from the National Science Foundation, began three years' work at the site. Our first step was to build a camp. In southern Mexico there are supposed to be two climatic seasons: a winter dry season, when it almost never

The Olmec ruler ensconced in the niche of a monolithic altar at La Venta holds a rope attached to the wrists of a seated captive.

rains, and the very wet summer. But in southern Veracruz some kind of moisture—drizzle, rain, or torrential downpour—is almost always falling. Shivering in our leaky tents, we found that fierce northers sweep down the Gulf Coast in winter, bringing cold drizzle and rain for days at a time. Until we put up houses with thatched roofs, we were a very soggy camp.

Our next job was to get San Lorenzo mapped. The picture that emerged after two seasons of surveying was very different from the one we had first imagined: San Lorenzo turned out to be one of the world's strangest archaeological sites.

The mesa, rising some 150 feet above the surrounding grass- and swamp-

covered plains, was originally considered to be a naturally formed plateau, the ravines being the result of erosion. Indeed, it must in large part be the result of geologic uplift by tectonic forces, most likely one of the deeply buried salt domes that are common in the northern half of the Isthmus of Tehuantepec. But San Lorenzo as we see it today has clearly been altered by the hand of ancient man. Reaching out like fingers on its north, west, and south sides are long, narrow ridges divided by the ravines. A pair of ridges on the western side exhibit bilateral symmetry, that is, every feature on one ridge is matched mirror-fashion by its counterpart; another such pair, divided by an asymmetric ridge, can be seen on the south side. This is hardly consistent with a natural origin.

Our excavations over three years demonstrated that the ridges are artificial, consisting of fill and cultural debris to a depth of at least twenty-five feet. Presumably, the first inhabitants—the Olmecs or their predecessors—took advantage of an already existing sand- and gravel-covered hill to carry out their plans. What could they have had in mind? As our map began to take shape, my first thought was that they might have been trying to construct a running or reclining animal on a titanic scale, three-quarters of a mile long, with its legs stretching north and south. But a subsequent mapping of the entire zone by aerial photography revealed much more of the total plan of San Lorenzo than our field map did. It showed a gigantic bird flying eastward, its extended wing feathers forming the ridges on the north and south, with its tail trailing to the west.

This may sound like poppycock, since such a grandiose plan could only have been appreciated from the air. Yet similar effigy mounds were erected by the early Adena and Hopewell cultures of our own midwestern states,

and the tremendous hilltop markings above the Peruvian deserts cannot be fully grasped from ground level either. My own guess is that some ancient Olmec ruler or priest (or both), inspired by cosmological ideas, ordered this construction on such a scale to impress the gods and men but that the plan was never completed.

There are several hundred earth mounds on the flat surface of San Lorenzo, but the site is not very impressive compared with such Meso-american giants as Teotihuacán or Tikal. At the center stands a very modest pyramid, probably once the sub-structure for a thatched-roof temple. Extending north and south of it are pairs of long mounds with narrow plazas between them. Presumably this was the focal point of San Lorenzo.

But was it an "empty" site, as we guess La Venta to have been, inhabited only by priestly bureaucrats and their entourages? Apparently not, for most of the two hundred structures are what we call house mounds: low, rectangular or ovoid platforms of earth designed to raise the pole and thatch houses of the commoners above the discomforts caused by summer (and winter) rains. A reasonable estimate of the ancient population might be a thousand persons, thus making Olmec San Lorenzo far from "empty."

When we arrived, there was no archaeological chronology for San Lorenzo, and we had to work one out for ourselves. This meant digging at least a dozen stratigraphic trenches and pits, peeling off layer by layer as we descended and segregating all broken pottery, stone tools, and other artifacts from each stratum. Having done this before at pre-Classic sites in coastal Guatemala, I was familiar with very early Mesoamerican pottery, but I was appalled by the number of pot-sherds—several hundred thousand in

This almost life-size figure of a wrestler flex-ing his heavy muscles is one of the few exam-ples of strict realism in Olmec sculpture.

all—that accumulated in our three seasons at San Lorenzo. This material has now been analyzed, and I have worked out a pre-Classic sequence consisting of seven distinct phases, or cultures, followed by a long period of abandonment (from around the time of Christ to about A.D. 900), and finally, a very late reoccupation by another, Toltec-like people.

But it is the pre-Classic period that concerns us here, for in that time span lies the story of the Olmecs at San Lorenzo. This is a story with dates, too, for we were fortunate enough to find well-preserved hearths or cooking fires with ample charcoal for radiocarbon analysis. It now seems that the first people to inhabit the San Lorenzo plateau arrived about 1500 B.C. They were not Olmecs, since their finely made pottery showed no signs of Olmec influence, but they may have been their ancestors. Two and a half centuries later, around 1250 B.C., there are signs that the people at San Lorenzo were beginning to take on Olmec character-istics: beautiful figurines of white clay show the unmistakable baby faces of the Olmecs, and there is much of the white-rimmed black pottery distinctive of the culture. Most important, we found a stone fragment that must have been part of a monumental carving of basalt.

The height of civilization in the area was reached in what we call the San Lorenzo phase, reliably dated to 1150–900 B.C. Here we are faced with remains that are undeniably Olmec, and it is also apparent that the site itself had reached its present form by that time. Olmec figurines of all sorts are found, some showing ball players wearing the heavy, padded belts and gloves typically used in that sacred game. Neither we nor Stirling found jade at San Lorenzo, which is curious since the Olmecs of La Venta were master jade carvers.

We are confident that the bulk of the fifty-eight known monuments at San Lorenzo were carved during the San Lorenzo phase. How do we know this?

Remember that Stirling found most of his stones lying in or near the ravines, obviously not in their original positions. One morning in March, 1967, I spotted a rough stone slab, or stela, sticking out of the ground in one of the western ridges and ordered that it be dug up. It was this modest excavation that enabled us to date the Olmec sculptures of San Lorenzo and to solve the riddle of their final disposition.

The stela in question appeared to be in its original position, and I wanted to establish its relationship to whatever strata might exist in the ridge. It soon became clear, however, that the work-man I had set at this task could not do his job within the limited excavation square I had measured off. Slightly to the north on the east-west ridge we started a new square, with the idea of enlarging the total work area. To my astonishment and delight we hit upon another sculpture, totally buried.

This turned out to be Monument 34, a magnificent, larger than life-size statue of a half-kneeling man in pure Olmec style. Like almost all other known Olmec monuments, this one had been mutilated before burial, in this case by having its head knocked off. At each shoulder was a disk, per-forated in the center, to which movable arms could be attached; whether they were of wood or stone we had no way of knowing.

Here, then, were two monuments, one just north of the other. If we con-tinued to excavate along the ridge in the same direction, mightn't we find a whole line of buried monuments? My guess was right. For weeks we dug on, uncovering one mutilated sculpture after another. And while following the same kind of lead west along another ridge, a second line of stones appeared, this time oriented east-west. Both "col-lections" produced a great variety of representations, ranging from a gigan-tic column embellished with a relief of a horrific werejaguar-god to a tiny carving of a fantastic spider. We now had strong evidence that a single

71

This white jade mask, incised with red marks symbolizing Olmec gods, was recently discovered in a riverbed in Arroyo Pesquero, Veracruz, with other objects. It shows signs of having been ritually burned.

monumental act of destruction had been inflicted on the Olmec sculptures of San Lorenzo. The iconoclasts had begun by smashing some monuments and pitting the features of others, sometimes by grinding axes on them. They had then dragged the objects of their fury onto specially prepared floors running along the ridges of the site, placed them carefully in long lines, and covered them with a special fill. Clearly, the stones found by Stirling in the ravines had *not* been pushed there by ancient hands but had slipped down, as the slope eroded, from their original positions in the ridges. This opened up the possibility that there might be a great many more stones still to be discovered.

Once we could associate the sculptures with archaeological strata, we were able to date them—or rather, date their final placement. From our study of the pottery and other artifacts lying on the floors and in the covering fill we learned that the great act of destruction took place no later than 900 B.C. But here again, we had settled one problem only to raise another: until now no archaeologist would have believed the Olmec sculptural style to be any older than 800 B.C. In the pe-

riod 1150–900 B.C., when we are positive our monuments were carved, the rest of Mesoamerica had not yet shown the first glimmerings of civilized life. Only at San Lorenzo did civilization burn brightly, with no antecedents yet discovered. Where did these people come from, with their culture already in full development?

The mysteries of San Lorenzo were tied up with more than the monuments. In one of the ridges we uncovered a troughlike stone, U-shaped in cross section. In his 1946 explorations Stirling had found a number of these lying jumbled at the bottom of one of the ravines, along with a like number of flat, rectangular stones, also of basalt. He surmised that the latter were covers for the troughs, which had once been fitted end to end to form a drain. He was right. On the edge of that same ravine, on the southwestern border of the San Lorenzo plateau, one of my laborers pointed out to me the end of just such a drain, still in place and deeply buried.

We excavated the drain completely during the final season, no simple task as it was covered with twelve to sixteen feet of overburden. A very remarkable system it was: a "main line" sloping down in an east-west direction and measuring 558 feet in length, with three subsidiary lines, totaling 98 feet, meeting the main line at a steep angle. From loose stones lying on the surface elsewhere, we are reasonably sure that another system, the mirror image to this one, lies on the southeast edge of the site.

What was the purpose of this drain, which represents no less than thirty tons of hard basalt? At its upper end there are openings for water to enter. Nearby, on the surface of the site, are several artificial ponds constructed by the Olmecs. We

have good reason to believe that during the San Lorenzo phase, when the drain system was put down, its starting point lay beneath the center of a large pond that was later covered up. Thus, it appears that the drain had no other function than to draw off water from the pond.

Since irrigation is unnecessary in the wet local climate, the ultimate function of this strange water-control system must have been purely ceremonial, perhaps connected with ritual bathing by the ancient Olmec leaders. Near the head of the drain we uncovered a remarkable statue of the Olmec rain god, complete with snarling, werejaguar face, while near its other end was a curious stone receptacle in the shape of a duck. The latter, discovered by Stirling, has an opening into which a trough-stone would fit perfectly.

What kind of a world did the Olmec leaders of San Lorenzo look out upon from their lofty plateau? Who owed them allegiance? Was theirs a tribal polity, ruled by chiefs, or a pristine state, dominated by kings? Since the

Olmecs of those times left no writing, we must rely on other lines of inquiry to answer these questions. But first let us consider the magnitude of the Olmec achievement at San Lorenzo three thousand years ago.

The site itself represents hundreds of thousands of tons of material—gravel, soil, sand, and rock—carried in by basketloads on men's backs. Similarly, the monuments must have required an army of laborers. Geological analysis has shown that the source of the basalt used in almost all the San Lorenzo monuments is the Cerro Cintepec, an extinct volcano some fifty miles north-northwest of San Lorenzo. The Colossal Heads average about eighteen tons, and one of the so-called altars weighs even more than that.

The Olmecs must have selected boulders of a suitable shape from the slopes of the volcano, somehow transporting them to the nearest navigable stream (no small distance) and then floating them to the mouth of the Coatza-coalcos River on balsa rafts. From there they would have been poled and pulled up the river to a point near San Lorenzo. Finally, each boulder would have been hauled up 150 feet, probably with ropes and simple rollers, to their final destination. We ourselves had some experience using simple materials and methods to move the monuments, and I can attest to the enormous effort required to move a ten-ton stone just one foot! It took fifty men with ropes and poles to set one Colossal Head upright. Thus, moving the larger monuments must have involved using more than a thousand workmen at a time.

Then there is the testimony of the persons represented by the stones. Scholars seem to agree that the Colossal Heads are portraits of Olmec rulers. Likewise, the seated figures in the niches of the "altars," shown either

The clay figure opposite depicts a baby with the pathological features of a Mongoloid idiot. Its special symbolism, if any, remains one of the mysteries of the Olmec civilization.

The rain god appears as a werejaguar, part human, part snarling beast. Concave at the back, the statue probably belonged to a system of water drains found at San Lorenzo.

with ropes holding captives or carrying the characteristic werejaguar infants, seem to depict real men. Great leaders, or their descendants, must have ordered the carving and setting up of these monuments—at what cost can only be imagined. Surely, then, we can postulate the existence of a polity that was more powerful than a mere tribal state.

But there is more. The existence of a political state implies a government with territorial jurisdiction not over a single tribe but over many. Whether an Olmec state can be postulated under this definition can never be fully determined, any more than it can be for *any* of the later civilizations of Mexico, other than the documented civilization of the Aztecs. Nevertheless, there is good reason to believe that the San Lorenzo Olmecs exerted an influence, political or otherwise, upon regions

as distant as the highlands of central and western Mexico, where Olmec pottery and even Olmec rock paintings have been discovered during the past few years.

But the most compelling evidence for San Lorenzo's high cultural and political status under the Olmecs comes from what at first glance might be thought an unlikely line of inquiry: ecology. Working within a sample area of about thirty square miles, centering on San Lorenzo, we are now trying to arrive at some idea of what the upper limit of human population may have been three thousand years ago. The extent of the sample area is probably that which would have been controlled by an agricultural tribe. If our population figure turns out to be much lower than the number of persons presumably involved in the construction and maintenance of the Olmec center, then San Lorenzo would have to have drawn labor and tribute from an area far greater than that of our sample.

Our calculation is based on the number of mouths that native systems of cultivation could have fed. It is not an easy one to make. Our preliminary studies strongly suggest, however, that the local population could never have constructed the artificial plateau and set up the monuments unaided. We may assume, then, that the Olmec rulers held sway over more than one tribe, and that they may, indeed, have exercised authority over much of southern Mexico.

One significant outgrowth of our study has been the work of Dr. Elizabeth S. Wing of the Florida State Museum, who has managed to identify scraps of bone contained in our Olmec rubbish heaps. The Olmecs were more finicky in their culinary habits than the present-day natives, who eat almost any kind of fish or game they can get their hands on. Olmec preferences, however, are curious, since the most common animals represented are snook (a large and good-tasting fish), man, marine toad, and turtle! We are not particularly bothered by the human remains, since cannibalism is well attested for the rest of Mesoamerica, but the toads are a puzzle, as they cannot be skinned without an extremely dangerous poison getting into the meat. We are now looking into the possibility that the Olmecs used them for a hallucinogenic substance called bufotenine, which is one of the active ingredients of the poison.

Far more significant, however, has been our research into local farming practices. The Olmecs, like all Mexican Indians, were basically corn eaters. Here we think that we may have hit upon the secret of the very early rise of native civilization in the San Lorenzo area. As in most of the world's tropical lands, the basic system of agriculture is of the shifting, or slash-and-burn, type, which means that a farmer will fell the trees or bush on a plot of land, burn them when dry, and continue to plant and harvest on the plot until declining yields or other factors force him to abandon it and search for another patch of forest.

One must also remember that there is a dry season and a rainy one. Most Mesoamerican farmers have only one major crop, planted with the first rains and harvested in the fall. On the gently rolling upland soils of the San Lorenzo area, however, there are *two* major crops, thanks to the winter northers, which keep the soil moist. Furthermore, in summer, when the rainstorms sweep daily across southwest Mexico, the winding, sluggish Coatzacoalcos River rises rapidly and covers all of the low-lying land with great sheets of water. San Lorenzo becomes a world afloat. As the rains taper off and the floods recede, the gift of the river is revealed: fresh mud and silt, deposited along the broad natural levees that flank the river.

These levees are classed by the natives as "prime land." While the upland areas tend to be communally owned, the levees are pretty much in private hands. Even though it is possible to cultivate only one crop on them, during the dry season, their pro-

duction is incredibly high for indigenous corn farming. As might be expected, those who bid for economic— and political—power in the village must gain effective control of the levee lands.

Was this, then, how the Olmecs rose to power and civilization more than three millenniums ago? We are reminded of ancient Egypt, so obviously tied to the rise and fall of its one great river. It is hardly a coincidence that most of the world's early civilizations have arisen in major river basins, and our Olmecs of San Lorenzo seem to have been no exception.

Every story has an end, or at least an epilogue. Olmec civilization did not come to a close after the massive destruction of San Lorenzo around 900 B.C. Curiously enough, La Venta seems to have reached the summit of its achievement immediately *after* this brutal event, and it may be that the overthrow of San Lorenzo's rulers was instigated by the leaders of that island citadel. Thereafter, the Olmec character of San Lorenzo was lost, for the pre-Classic reoccupations that continued until the beginning of the Christian Era lack the art style that is the Olmec hallmark.

Eventually, even La Venta was destroyed, and perhaps its successor, Tres Zapotes. But Olmec civilization became transformed into some of the other brilliant civilizations of Mesoamerica's Classic period. The farther back we trace the Classic cultures of Mexico and Central America, the more characteristic of the Olmecs they seem to become.

The most clear-cut case for an Olmec heritage is presented by the famous Mayan civilization of the Classic period. It may seem a far cry from the earth or adobe constructions of the Olmecs to the towering pyramid-temples of the Mayas, but a closer look at Mayan art and learning reveals much in common. Take the day-to-day calendar system called the Long Count. Although for many decades scientists

A brooding male figure here cradles the symbolic werejaguar. This statue was recently stolen from a Mexican museum by art thieves.

considered this a Mayan invention, Stirling and others have shown that it had far earlier roots in Olmec country. There is now good reason to believe that the well-known writing system of the Mayas may be of Olmec origin as well. Based on what we know of the earliest Classic Mayan art and culture, the Mayas themselves may, indeed, once have been Olmec, moving in the centuries before the Christian Era eastward into the jungles of Yucatán and Guatemala.

Strong Olmec influence may also be detected in the Oaxaca highlands of Mexico, where the Zapotec people held sway. Kent Flannery of the University of Michigan has recently identified a local Oaxaca culture that was either importing Olmec products or making very good imitations of them, and Olmec artistic traits are to be found in the well-known Danzante reliefs, the strange stone carvings of slain men erected at the great Zapotec site of Monte Albán.

The list could be expanded to encompass most early civilizations of Mexico and Central America. The Olmecs seem to be behind all of them—an ancient, shadowy, "mother culture" whose own origins remain shrouded in mystery even to this day.

Professor of anthropology at Yale, Michael D. Coe is the author of several books on pre-Columbian civilizations and has made a number of important archaeological discoveries in the field as well.

PORTRAIT: BIBLIOTHÈQUE NATIONALE—GIRAUDON; OPPOSITE: ANTOINE FRANÇOIS PRÉVOST, *L'Histoire du Chevalier des Grieux et de Manon Lescaut*, 1839

Perfide Manon and Abbé Prévost

She was the classic cocotte,
he the classic dupe;
first the Abbé wrote his famous
story, and
then he set out to live it

Abbé Prévost, a sometime priest, wears a gentlemanly wig in a contemporary portrait.

While most of the noble and the good are forgotten, naughty Manon Lescaut lives in our minds, accompanied by faint strains from Massenet and Puccini. *Perfide Manon!* She could remain faithful to her Chevalier only twelve days; yet she is the symbol of love all-compelling. She is Venus Libertina, the goddess of pleasure; she is also Kali, the bloodsucker, the goddess of destruction.

Her creator is known in literary history simply as Abbé Prévost. His life has been explored by a number of acute researchers, of whom the latest are Claire-Eliane Engel and Professor Frédéric Deloffre of the Sorbonne. The author was born Antoine François Prévost, in Hesdin, northern France, on All Fools' Day, 1697, by one of fate's little jokes. His forebears were well-to-do government officials with pretensions to gentility. He was educated in a good Jesuit school, but quitted it at sixteen to join the army.

Four years later, he reappears, to enter the Jesuit order as a novice. Although his seminary record was excellent, he changed his mind and left his studies to rejoin the army with an officer's commission. Again he shifted course. What he discreetly terms "the unhappy conclusion of a too tender relationship" made him seek anew the consolations of the religious life. In November, 1721, he took his vows in the Benedictine monastery of Jumièges. Shortly after, he was transferred to the famous Paris abbey of Saint-Germain-des-Prés, and, later, was ordained.

The monks of Saint-Germain were chiefly devoted to scholarship, at that moment to the production of a gigantic history of the French church, the *Gallia Christiana.* The labors pleased the author that cohabited with the soldier and the monk in Prévost's spirit. But there was another occupant, lusty and wanton, who could not forget the "too tender relationship" and the soldier's easy pleasures.

He began to write a novel, of frenzied passion and bloodcurdling adventures. He must have presented an edifying picture to his superiors as he sat walled with mighty folios, scribbling away at what was presumed to be the *Gallia Christiana.* He called his novel *Mémoires et aventures d'un homme de qualité.* Four small volumes were published in 1728, with notable success in the world, if not in the monastery. The author then asked papal authority to transfer to a less austere establishment of the Benedictine rule. An apostolic brief was granted, but its validation in France was held up while the authorities investigated.

Impatient, the Abbé fled the convent, doffed his gown, and resumed the costume and sword of a gentleman. His ecclesiastical superiors obtained a *lettre de cachet* for his arrest. In this document he is described as being of middle height, blond, with wide-set blue eyes, full face, and ruddy complexion. He now proposed to turn Protestant. He obtained from the chaplain of the Dutch embassy a letter of introduction to the Archbishop of Canterbury, presenting himself as an interesting convert. He may have been moved by the knowledge that the English court pensioned Catholic refugees ripe for conversion. In November, 1728, he took ship for England.

In London the interesting convert used his letters and his charm to establish himself. He found lodgment as tutor to the son of Sir John Eyles, eminent in the business and political worlds. In his household Prévost remained for two years, touring southern England and writing.

This happy situation was suddenly ended, according to contemporary gossips, by an *affaire de coeur.* Specifically, it was whispered that the ex-priest aspired to marry Sir John Eyles's only daughter, and that the proud Englishman bought him off and had him banished from the realm.

In any case, the Abbé removed hurriedly from England to Holland in the autumn of 1730. He established himself in The Hague, center of the book trade, and gave himself up to a rage of production. It was one of those periods of heightened tension, familiar in literary lives, when the words flow faster than the pen can follow. He added two volumes to the *Mémoires d'un homme de qualité,* wrote four volumes of a new novel, *Cleveland,* began a translation into French of De Thou's monumental Latin history of sixteenth-century France, and produced his immortal *Manon Lescaut.* He describes his own masterpiece as "depicting the results of a violent passion which renders reason useless when unhappily one surrenders totally to it—a passion which, being incapable of completely stifling in the heart the sentiments of virtue, prevents one from practicing it."

In the heat of creation he met a person who rendered reason useless, who

By MORRIS BISHOP

prevented him from practicing the precepts of virtue. Her name was Lenki Eckhardt. Prévost refers to her as "a lady of merit and good birth who had suffered reverses of fortune." Others describe her as "a veritable leech who had bled white most of her lovers," and identify some of her victims. She was the classic cocotte, and Prévost, for all his literary sagacity, the classic dupe. He broke with his friends in Dutch society, or they broke with him. Money seemed somehow to disappear; he was forced to borrow and to beg his publishers for advances.

Soon he stood on the edge of bankruptcy. No doubt he would have chosen to rescue himself by hard work and economy, and no doubt scornful Lenki counseled flight to befool the creditors. Prévost succeeded in wheedling 1,700 florins—a handsome sum for an author at any time—from his publishers, and the couple departed for England, probably early in January, 1733. The Abbé's debts were accounted at 2,500 florins; his abandoned furniture and possessions were sold for 550 florins, leaving the creditors deep in the hole.

In London the Dutch florins were spent by summer, and pecunious friends were evasive. Prévost founded a magazine, Le Pour et Contre, to convey to Paris the literary news of London. The idea was a good one, but the returns negligible. It was perhaps Lenki who suggested a recourse. Prévost possessed a letter from his former pupil, Francis Eyles, in which the careless youth had left a wide gap between "Your humble servant" and his signature. Prévost had only to clip off the letter's text, write in the vacant space "Pay 50 pounds to M. Prévost or to his order," and present the document at a bank for payment.

But retribution duly followed. On December 11, 1733, Prévost was jailed in Gatehouse Prison on the complaint of Francis Eyles. The matter was serious; forgery was a hanging crime. But young Eyles, probably recoiling at sending his old tutor to a shameful death, withdrew his complaint, and the Abbé was discharged. One suspects

that the father, Sir John Eyles, made it a condition of his release that he should get out of England and stay out.

Never leave a blank space above your signature.

Prévost ventured back to France, and was there joined by Lenki, faithful in her fashion. He pulled what strings were in his grasp and obtained (on June 5, 1734) an apostolic brief that pardoned him for his misdeeds but directed him to another branch of the Benedictine order at Évreux. After only three months of expiation he returned to Paris, to edit Le Pour et Contre, write a series of novels, and

Prévost's heroine, Manon, dies in her ruined lover's arms in the "desert" of Louisiana.

cultivate the great who kept open house for the intelligentsia. He assumed the *petit collet,* the clerical collar, and was appointed chaplain to the Prince de Conti, with his quarters provided. He received no salary, but gained security against hounding creditors and made friends in the world of letters, among them Voltaire and Rousseau.

And Lenki? We hear no more of her, unless by chance she was the Mme de Chester who, to Prévost's great relief, left Paris in November, 1735, and got married. He dowered her with his last eight hundred francs.

Freed of Lenki and Mme de Chester (perhaps in the same person), Prévost began to prosper. Literature and patronage conferred excellent rewards.

He was enabled to rent a pleasant house on the outskirts of Paris, with a garden, a lackey, a cook, and a charming widow as housekeeper. He was even in a position to buy a *Holy Family* by Veronese for 6,600 francs.

A true writer never stops writing. He produced novels of his own, and translated those of Samuel Richardson, which had a splendid sale. (There is no indication that the author received any payment.) He edited and wrote a great collection of voyages. Altogether, he published 112 volumes, 65 of them original, the rest translations. He died on November 25, 1763, of an apoplectic stroke, while taking a walk in the woods of Chantilly.

Of all Prévost's work, *Manon Lescaut* stands apart and above. It is a tense and moving recital of doomed love, a lyric ready for music. Prévost describes his hero, the Chevalier des Grieux, as the slave of love, who foresees his misfortunes but hasn't the strength to forestall them, who thinks well but acts badly. The Chevalier surrenders all—position, fortune, honor—for his Manon. For her he becomes a thief, a blackmailer, and a murderer. She loves him, too, but she loves pleasure, comfort, and pretty things more. Even in her obliviousness of morality, she retains something pure and maidenly. Like the Chevalier, we love her still, in spite of all.

It was long presumed that the story was a transposition of the Abbé's subjection to Lenki. Many of the scenes—of the gentleman's home in Artois, of the Amiens inn, of seminary life, of the gaming rooms of the Hôtel de Transylvanie, of prison routine—are taken from life. But recent investigators have proved beyond question that the book was written and in print before Prévost met Lenki. *Manon* is therefore not a record but a forecast. Prévost recognized the possibilities in his nature, and he turned them into fact. No doubt he aided his fate, accepting the foreseen direction and guiding it when choices, little or big, had to be made. He made his life fulfill his art.

SELF-PORTRAIT, 1970

FRANCIS BACON:
A
RETROSPECTIVE
AND
A PREVIEW

Some find a pervasive sense of terror, isolation and morbidity in his work. But England's greatest painter would answer that his images are nothing less than a "history of Europe in our century"

Francis Bacon's self-portrait, left, and the photograph above were both made in 1970. Bacon portrays himself before a glowing canvas and has laid open his own countenance in a characteristic swirl. The torso has seemingly vanished inside the overcoat; the legs emerge from the seat of the chair. The portrait has not yet been exhibited and is here reproduced for the first time.

By JOHN RUSSELL

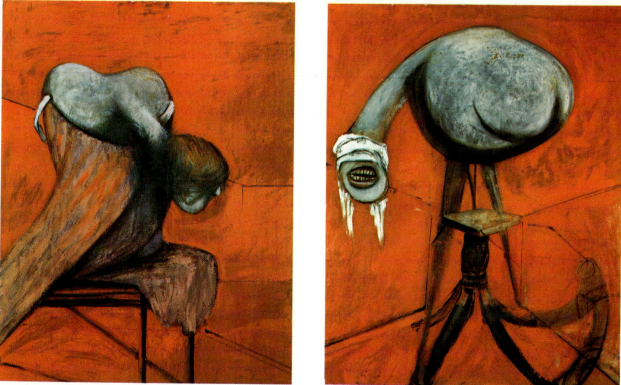

Three Studies for Figures at the Base of a Crucifixion, 1944

One would find it difficult to make a list of what Britain has given to the world since 1945 and not put the work of Francis Bacon somewhere near the top. Bacon's paintings have made their mark in two related but quite separate ways. They present, on the one hand, an index of contemporary attitudes: anyone who wants to know what it felt like to be alive after World War II will find in Bacon's paintings an account as accurate as any to be had in postwar poetry or drama or fiction. And on the other hand, these same paintings speak for the continuation of monumental figure painting as it has been practiced in Europe, though not often in England, for four hundred years and more. In paintings of this order, man is the measure of all things, and oil paint on canvas the finest of his instruments.

It took some time for all this to be acknowledged. In the late 1940's Bacon aroused attention primarily for the ambiguous and often sinister quality of his subject matter. Something of this

still remains: every encyclopedia of modern art will tell you that Bacon specializes in "undefinable horror" and that "the isolation and terror of the human condition have been his continuing theme." But when the first major retrospective of his work was held at the Tate Gallery in 1962, the impression it left with Londoners was anything but morbid; we felt, on the contrary, as if one of the great ages of painting had been born anew and we had just walked through room after room in which our immediate ancestors were portrayed with a virile energy and a commanding sense of design.

Of course, there were paradoxes and contradictions in this. But there have always been paradoxes and contradictions in Francis Bacon's career. He was born in Dublin on October 28, 1909, and when he was carried to the baptismal font, it was to be given a name already illustrious in British history. Doubtless his parents meant well; but to an unambitious man a great name is a nuisance, and to an ambitious person

it is a handicap. Unlucky the man who is today born Beethoven, born Shakespeare, born Cézanne. Such names dwarf their bearers. All comparisons are to their disadvantage, and they know that every time they come into the room someone will say to himself, "Ah, what a falling-off!"

So the auguries were none too good for the newborn Bacon who was named Francis in the fall of 1909. Francis Bacon (1561–1626) was one of the greatest Englishmen of all time. There were flaws in his character, just as there were flaws in his achievement; but as a statesman, as a philosopher, as a lawyer, as a scientist, as a master of English prose, and as an undeluded student of society, he exerts, even today, a wayward fascination. Bacon had the kind of peremptory magic that, once experienced, is never forgotten; if our world rewards the plodding specialist, the Elizabethan world admired a man like Bacon, the dazzling freewheeler. He had an omnivorous, multivalent curiosity. If sharp reverses came his way,

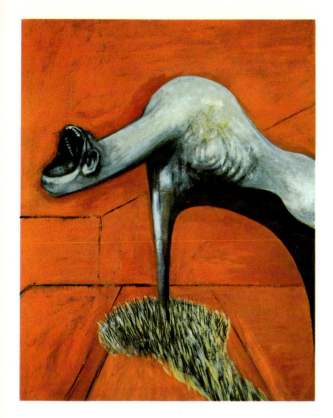

This triptych of monsters, horribly denuded, one faceless, one bandaged, one on what seems to be a bed of nails, was first shown in London in April, 1945, just before the end of World War II, and it caused a tremendous stir. In traditional iconography, three women, one of them the mother of Jesus, mourn at the foot of the Cross. Bacon's trio, however, is not at the Crucifixion but a crucifixion, and he has also referred to them as the Eumenides—the three Greek Furies who hound unpunished criminals.

he turned them to good account; and when an idea presented itself, he pursued it to the end, irrespective of where it would lead him. He knew the world, and he was Lord Chancellor at a time when that office meant even more than it does today; but he was also at home, as much as any Englishman of his day, with ideas.

Francis Bacon (b. 1909) is also at home in the world of ideas, and as it happens, he is a collateral descendant of Francis Bacon (b. 1561). But at any time between 1909 and 1945 it would have seemed quite implausible that he would one day dominate the imagination of his time to a degree that even his great ancestor might have envied. Bacon II, as I shall momentarily call him, had none of the outward advantages of Bacon I. Bacon I went to the best college in Cambridge at the age of twelve; Bacon II had no formal schooling at all. Bacon I was the son of Sir Nicholas Bacon, Lord Keeper of England, who entertained Queen Elizabeth I in his house at Gorhambury;

Bacon II was the son of a horse trainer. Before he was twenty-four, Bacon I was a member of Parliament and the author of a "Letter of Advice to Queen Elizabeth" that showed him to have the makings of a farsighted and most ingenious statesman. At the same age, Bacon II was a drifter with no clear bent for anything. Bacon I lived all his life within the periphery of power, and at a time when power was most imperious; Bacon II sets private affection above all things, and would never go anywhere or see anyone merely for the sake of "importance."

Even so, the antithesis defeats itself. Bacon II is a much more complex character than he has so far appeared. He may have had no formal education, but he can get at the heart of a new book as fast as anyone at Oxford. His father may have been a horse trainer, but he had very good connections: Bacon grew up in an Anglo-Irish society that was anything but plebeian. (Queen Victoria

once encouraged his grandfather to claim the lapsed title of Lord Oxford, which was rightfully his, but he declined on the grounds that he was too poor to live up to it.) Bacon never went to art school, but he can get all the training he needs from studying the old masters. He is completely without pretensions, yet I have never seen anyone, in any walk of life, who did not instinctively defer to him. To quote Mallarmé on Whistler, he comes across as *"un monsieur rare, Prince en quelque chose."*

Francis Bacon admits of no compromise, either in life or in art. He never says what he doesn't think, and if a choice of actions presents itself, he unalterably does whatever will serve the best interests of his work. He has an openhanded sociability and is at home in all societies, but in bondage to none of them. If he means to be in the studio at nine o'clock in the morning, he will be there, no matter how late and how deep the potations of the night before. He brings the same easy directness to his relations with every-

FIGURE IN A LANDSCAPE, 1945

These three paintings, chosen from Bacon's earlier works, project a malaise that few other painters have ever tried to convey. Figure in a Landscape *has connotations of war—a headless marksman with a machine gun.* Painting, 1946 *features a butchered carcass and an umbrella sheltering someone whose face is all mouth (an image possibly derived from photographs of the shouting Mussolini).* Dog *shows an animal braced against, or for, some final assault. Bacon's paintings are perhaps too easily turned into vehicles for psychic explorations; but where paranoia and fear are present, his images reinforce them almost beyond endurance.*

one, whether it be "the highest in the land" or someone just out of jail. I cannot improve here on what I wrote about Bacon nearly ten years ago: "Routine, convention and pretence have no part in his life. He is one of England's rare great serious readers; and if the talk skirts a subject which really engages his interest the pulpy, convivial, youthful-seeming face turns into an iron mask of concentration and his companions see that the half-truths with which they themselves would be satisfied strike him as loathsome and contaminated. He risks himself for truth, in conversation, as completely as he risks himself in the studio. He thinks everything through; and if his conclusions differ from those of his friends he presents them with an even politeness that does not exclude the total destruction of another's point of view. The subject is too serious, we infer, and friendship too stable, for anyone to take offence. . . ."

Now, one could be all of these things and still be no good as a painter. England is, or was, full of forthright old persons who can distinguish what is good from what isn't, and are yet quite unable to carry this over into their own activities. Bacon's is one of the very rare cases in which strength of character is not enfeebled in the work. There was a time, early in his career, when this was not so: "I do not exist for the critic before 1945," he now likes to say.

Bacon in the 1930's was known to a few people as a potentially remarkable person with a gift for calculated drifting. He was in with one or two people who knew about painting, but he was also in with some—in London, Paris, Berlin —who led an unstructured life and had what the police call "no visible means of support." He made tubular furniture at one time; a rug designed by him came up at Sotheby's not long ago; there was once in existence a London apartment decorated by him. He gambled a great deal and was rumored to have worked for a short time as a gen-

tleman's gentleman, only to lose this post when his employer found him dining at the next table at the Ritz Hotel. One or two elderly connoisseurs took an interest in his paintings in the 1930's, and in 1937 he was one of the "Young British Painters" who were shown by the old-master house of Thomas Agnew & Sons. But it was not until World War II that his apparently aimless existence suddenly assumed its definitive shape.

Bacon has always been asthmatic, and in World War II he was excused even from the unexacting civil-defense duties to which he was assigned for a time. Almost without his knowing how, or when, or where the initial precipitation occurred, he realized that the only thing that interested him was to begin to paint, as he later put it, "the history of Europe in our century." He did this not in narrative style but in an elliptic, ambiguous way: it was part of his ambition that "the story should not talk louder than the paint." The history in question was not to come

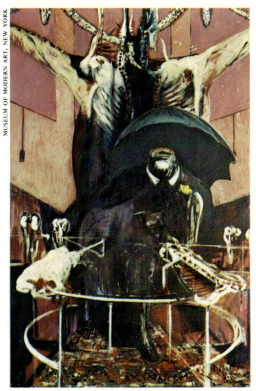

PAINTING, 1946

DOG, 1952

through to us "in a long diatribe through the brain," it was to come across "directly, on to the nervous system."

He first succeeded in this with the *Three Studies for Figures at the Base of a Crucifixion,* which were painted in 1944 and were shown in London in April, 1945. They came at the very time that people were congratulating themselves on the fact that as far as World War II was concerned, the worst was over. It wasn't, of course: the news about Belsen and Dachau was less than two months away, and in the light of that news, and of the general situation of postwar Europe, Bacon's three figures now strike us as a straightforward, incomparably vivid evocation of the ghoulishness that prompts people to hurry to the scene of human disaster and, once there, stay to gloat. But in April, 1945, people saw them as gratuitously spooky: as specters to be dismissed as soon as possible.

The figures had their spooky side, undeniably. Their anatomy equipped them to probe, bite, and suck, but their functioning in other respects was mysterious. At least two of them were sightless, and one was unpleasantly bandaged: all this at a time when romantic landscapes and idealized plowboys were the mainstay of British art. You had to look at the small print in our newspapers—then much given to jubilation—to realize that Bacon had given poetic expression to truths that were no less real for being unpalatable: victory had its hideous side, and good news an obverse that froze the blood.

If the three figures looked sensational in 1945, that was no fault of their creator. Bacon has never tried to be sensational. But neither has he evaded the facts of our time. For a number of years those facts were presented in his paintings in a form that owed much to the newsreel, the news magazine, and that novelty of the day, the candid camera. This in its turn was interpreted by some people as an opportunistic practice, whereas in reality it was prompted by the wish both to master such new forms of imagery as were being offered and to achieve in paint the same immediacy of news photography. Bacon had noticed that in candid-camera images the public had accepted a degree of distortion that it was still most unwilling to accept in a painting. In wartime Europe appearances were remade by the picture magazines in a way that painting had yet to catch up with; and these remade appearances were all the more telling for being more abrupt, more violent, and more psychologically disturbing than any previously recorded in the mass media. If the protective wrappings were being taken off life, it was not painting's job to put them back on.

Bacon spends a great deal of his time daydreaming, and many of his daydreams have to do with the vast repertory of already-existing images that he keeps in his London studio. Books by the hundred and magazines by the thousand have been torn apart over the years: pages from a book on cave painting lie next to a newspaper image of one of Hitler's massacres, and

VINCENT VAN GOGH: THE PAINTER
ON THE ROAD TO TARASCON, 1888

*"The real painters do not paint things as they
are.... They paint them as they themselves feel
them to be,"* wrote Van Gogh in 1885. Van
Gogh's self-portrait, above, destroyed during
World War II, is a work Bacon particularly
likes. In 1957, inspired by a reproduction in a
book, he paid it homage by doing a series of sun-
struck variations, one of which appears at right.

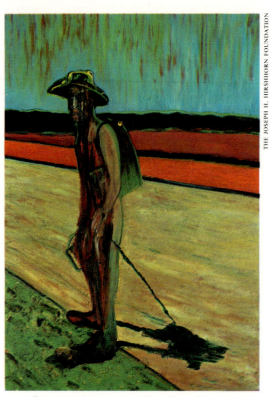

STUDY FOR PORTRAIT OF VAN GOGH V, 1957

a reproduction of a work by Velázquez next to a big-game hunter's photograph of a rhinoceros in long grass. If he got up a tremendous head of steam in the late 1940's, it was partly because he was suddenly able to deal with material that had been piling up in his mind for a quarter of a century. Bacon's life span is contemporaneous with some of the most terrible moments of human history, and he has relived them in his imagination, more intensely even than many of those who were actually present at the time. His object is not to exploit those moments, but to come to terms with them.

The best way of coming to terms with them was to submit them to the procedures of aesthetics. Art can deal with violence of a kind that in life would be merely degrading. The events of *Oedipus Rex*, or of *Macbeth* or *King Lear*, would corrupt and brutalize if we witnessed them in life; what gives them exaltation is what Paul Valéry called "the honor of mankind, St. Language." In painting, equally, the old

masters, with their scenes of martyrdom and massacre, reconcile us to events that would be sickening if we came across them in the street: Poussin's *Rape of the Sabines*, for instance, or his *Massacre of the Innocents* (a great favorite with Bacon, by the way).

How to do the same after World War II? That was Bacon's problem. Initially he solved it by presenting eccentric or ambiguous subject matter in a comparatively straightforward way. We could, for instance, remake the subject matter of the Museum of Modern Art's *Painting, 1946* into a *tableau vivant:* a figure with a gaping mouth, an umbrella, a carcass from the butcher's, and we would be well provided. It was in part because of this that people were so quick to settle for a single interpretation of these early paintings. The open mouth, for instance, that appears in so many of them: how convenient if that open mouth could be interpreted once and for all as a soundless scream! It could then be "placed" for all eternity as a late variant of Munch's fa-

mous image of the 1890's. Here would be, once again, a symbol for the unfocused anguish that poisons the wells of the inner life: striking, of course, but we've seen it before.

As a matter of fact, Bacon does not see his paintings as horrific and, in particular, does not agree that the open mouths he paints are necessarily open in a scream. An involuntary yawn, a manic hilarity, a mindless good-fellowship, an off-the-record confidence, or the silence of total hebetude—all are possible alternatives, and all are valid. "Rembrandt unlocks the valves of feeling," Bacon once said, "but he doesn't necessarily say anything specific." Just as we no longer believe in the monolithic pre-Freudian concept of personality, so it is childish to expect to interpret major paintings of the 1960's and 1970's as we do the works of Winslow Homer.

It did gradually get through to people, as exhibition followed exhibition, that in Bacon's work the valves of feeling were being unlocked as much by

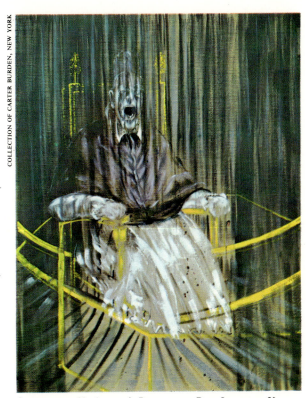

STUDY AFTER VELÁZQUEZ'S PORTRAIT OF POPE INNOCENT X, 1953

VELÁZQUEZ: POPE INNOCENT X, 1650

Velázquez is perhaps the painter Bacon most reveres; and the famous portrait of Pope Innocent X, done in 1650, is one of Bacon's obsessions. In the early 1950's he began a series of variations on this masterwork. The shrieking pope at left, painted in 1953, is one of these. Most viewers see it as a symbol of decay, of Authority gone mad; yet its debt to the original is clear, and Bacon's pope has his own dignity.

the paint itself as by the subject matter. Nor was that subject matter uniformly disquieting. In the early 1950's Bacon began to paint voluptuous figures of a kind that had almost gone out of style in modern times. Moreover, Bacon was totally committed to putting his best energies on the line—time after time attempting new achievements in ways that courted failure but never accepted it.

All this was done in the interest of greater veracity, but it was also done in the name of something that has lately had fewer and fewer defenders: painting. The period from 1945 to 1971 was one in which old-style oil-painting-on-canvas got more and more of a bad name among the people who habitually comment on art. Those ponderous old colors, so slow to dry! Those images laboriously made by hand when more up-to-date expedients now abound! How thick-witted to stick to a medium in which everything has been said!

Bacon has, of course, heard this a thousand times, and I suspect that it does not altogether displease him to be one of the last men in the world who pins his faith absolutely and entirely on the traditional methods of oil painting. He never makes drawings. He despises prints. He thought of doing sculpture at one time not long ago, but nothing came of it, though he has not entirely discarded the idea. He knows that acrylic paints take much of the drudgery out of painting, and much of the risk; but as he welcomes the risk and does not resent the drudgery, the bright immediate sparkle and the deadened echoes of synthetic paint have very little hold upon him. He will no more analyze his technical methods than he will visit a fortuneteller: "Why should I inhibit the play of instinct?" He goes to every exhibition of consequence, even if the work on view revolts him, just as he looks at every shop window on the street, even if the look turns into a glare that could turn a shopman to stone. He believes in the

unique power of oil paint to work directly upon the nervous system, and for nothing in the world would he barter that power.

In the 1950's he didn't mind how explicit his allusions to the great paintings of the past were: if he invoked a Velázquez or a Van Gogh, he invoked it directly and unmistakably, and he seldom made use of living sitters. Velázquez's portrait of Pope Innocent X had a manifold interest for Bacon. It was a key work in the career of an artist who has never been surpassed as a recorder of fact. It was about what uniforms do to human beings: Bacon turned to it at a time when for twenty years a great part of European life had been lived in uniforms of one kind or another. And it was about the very curious fact that over a large area of the earth's surface, absolute power had been wielded, and to a certain degree is still wielded, by a man in drag, a skirted tyrant whose ritual gestures stand for Authority but whose gestures can also be interpreted, if we are so minded,

PORTRAIT OF GEORGE DYER AND LUCIAN FREUD, 1967

PORTRAIT OF ISABEL RAWSTHORNE
STANDING IN A STREET IN SOHO, 1967

as indications of infantile regression.

The relationship of Bacon and Van Gogh is less easy to read, and the results of the involvement seem to me to be unsuccessful as often as not. But when Van Gogh painted himself on the road to Tarascon in blazing sunshine, he produced an unforgettable image of the artist as a beast of burden: the artist is bound to his painting materials as Joan of Arc was bound to the stake. Bacon may have wished, consciously or not, to keep this image alive—especially since the original was destroyed during World War II.

Recently, his ever-growing confidence has allowed him either to subsume such allusions or to dispense with them completely. Painting after painting in the 1960's was the consummation of an idiosyncratic idea long nurtured. A small cast of his friends has been called upon to mimic the dramas of "Europe in this century"; and Bacon II has ventured as deeply as Bacon I into the penetralia of human motives. In so doing, he has developed new ways of presenting the human image. "In Shakespeare's day," he said not long ago, "it meant a great deal when Hamlet made his speech about 'To be or not to be.' The alternatives were absolute. But today we ask of art that it should show us what it is like 'to be *and* not to be' at one and the same time. That's the problem we must set ourselves."

In practical terms, the pursuit of "to be and not to be" means the invention of forms that both conform and do not conform to our everyday experience of the human body. It means allying the strongest possible dose of verifiable reality to the strongest possible dose of inspired risk. The painter must have one foot on ground that is common to us all, and the other on ground that no one has essayed before. Without the one, the picture could not be read; without the other, it would be at best a meritorious remake of an earlier painting. "The moment you know what to do," Bacon said lately, "you're just making another sort of illustration."

If Bacon has often turned to portraiture in these last years, it is in part because it now constitutes such a desperate adventure. "You simply can't bring off a portrait today. You're asking chance to fall your way *all the time.* The paint has to slide into appearance at every level, and the accidents have to be all in your favor." Most of the people he has painted in this context share his own preference for risks run consciously, and for the notion of destiny as something to be outwitted for as long as possible. Free-spoken, instinctive, unprevaricating, they are slack-wire walkers who disdain the safety net; and since Bacon is still associated by many people with squalor and depravity, it is worth saying that the portraits of Isabel Rawsthorne in particular are an acknowledgment of all that is staunchest and most generous in human nature. The portraits are not lifelike, but they are like life. The eye fixes us with an unforgettable urgency; the way the hair sits on the scalp, the double tunnel of

PORTRAIT OF GEORGE DYER RIDING A BICYCLE, 1966

The portraits shown opposite and at right are of Bacon's close friends: George Dyer; Lucian Freud, grandson of Sigmund and himself a gifted painter; and Isabel Rawsthorne, the wife of the composer Alan Rawsthorne. Bacon regards portraits as almost magical objects, but he also regards portraiture as an act of violence against the sitter. As he says, he is interested in transcending the documentary element, not in making conventional representations of a face.

the nostrils, the interlocking of color and substance in flesh that is thoroughly aroused—all these things come out, and in ways that make words like "distortion" seem quite ridiculous.

I myself especially prize the *Portrait of Isabel Rawsthorne Standing in a Street in Soho* of 1967. Transposed into masculine terms, that proud, watchful figure could be a great sea-going captain on leave: a lifelong single-handed adventurer stepping out from a blue-awninged restaurant after an unusually good luncheon, with a rakish open roadster of antique design drawn up at the curb and a searching, unembarrassed glance at the small crowd that has gathered to see him drive off. A far cry, all this, from the nightmare figures with which Bacon made his name in 1945, but the career that is soon to be celebrated at the Grand Palais in Paris has covered the extremes of human nature and been as trenchant at the beginning as it is now.

Bacon still deals with violence where violence is implicit in the subject: in paraphrases, for instance, of one or two celebrated crimes, or in the bullfight series that he undertook a year or two ago. But he came to dislike the bullfight paintings because the subject matter was already so dramatic that it did not lend itself to further heightening. Among his late work, the ones he likes best, I think, are those that relate to classic European subjects, like the *Two Men Working,* with its echoes of the French nineteenth century, or the *Lying Figure in Mirror,* which once again harks back to a classic European picture subject: the extent to which human beings are completed, or betrayed, or simply traduced by the image of themselves that a mirror throws back at them. Bacon in these paintings is not out to "make another Bacon" but rather to continue a certain adventure.

The first Francis Bacon may not have written the plays of Shakespeare, as some of his admirers claim, but the second Francis Bacon has painted—and who could have done it better?—the "history of Europe in our century." He has done this not in economic or political terms but with poetic human images, single or grouped, that stand for life as it has had to be lived by millions of people. In that life, jailer and jailed change places, as do the torturer and his victim. Constant, on the other hand, is the role of the onlooker, who, whether from indifference, laziness, or an unrepressed inclination to gloat, sees hideous things done and himself does nothing to prevent them. Against all this can be set the survival of one or two robust and agile individuals; and they, too, find their memorial in Bacon.

John Russell is the art critic of the Sunday Times *of London, and the author of books on Seurat, Matisse, Max Ernst, and Henry Moore. His book on·Francis Bacon will be published this fall in London by Thames and Hudson and in the U.S. by the New York Graphic Society.*

FOR A SELECTION OF BACON'S NEWEST PAINTINGS, TURN THE PAGE

Three Studies of the Male Back, 1970

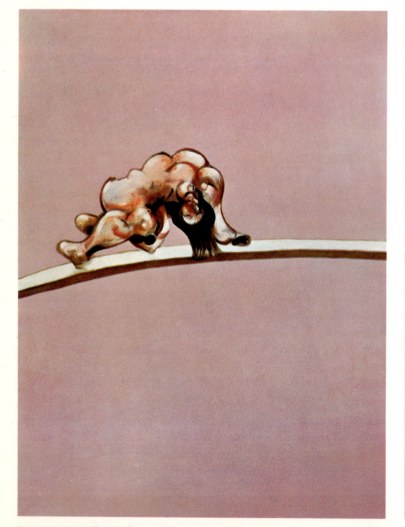

Studies of the Human Body, 1970

PAINTINGS FOR THE GRAND PALAIS

The paintings in this portfolio, all recently completed and none previously exhibited, are shown here for the first time and will be seen at the Grand Palais in Paris, beginning October 26, in a retrospective exhibition that will include 130 of Bacon's canvases. He is the first English painter ever to be honored by the French government with a show on this scale. Asked to name the most important living artists (excluding the established modern masters Picasso, Chagall, Ernst, and Miró), a recent worldwide poll of art critics and museum directors ranked Bacon at the top.

After seeing *Three Studies of the Male Back,* one of the two monumental triptychs shown here, in Bacon's studio, John Russell wrote: "In the two outer panels, a man shaving himself with his back to us is reflected in a magnifying mirror just above his head. In the central panel the mirror is blacked out . . . The three backs are the main subject of the painting, and they are most sumptuously rendered, with the kind of 'male voluptuousness' that Bacon admires in Michelangelo." Of the second triptych, showing a female figure, Mr. Russell pointed out that the forms are sculptural: "In particular the chunky central figure put many observers in mind of an antique torso cut off at the top of the thighs. Above the massive breasts and shoulders was an umbrella, dark green against the palest of pink backgrounds; and where the face could have been Bacon put in an ambiguous form which was derived . . . from a photograph of a bird diving out of the sky . . ."

The paintings here and on the pages that follow show Bacon's continuing preoccupation with the human figure, with the portrait, with the perfecting of old motifs (the umbrella, the butchered beef, the hidden face) that have pervaded his work from the beginning. One subject, that of the bullfight, is entirely new. Though not himself an aficionado, Bacon was drawn to the image because of its violent motion and the risks that must be decided upon and taken in the bull ring.

STUDY FOR PORTRAIT, 1970

Two Men Working in a Field, 1971

LYING FIGURE IN MIRROR, 1971

Second Version of Painting, 1946, in Museum of Modern Art, 1971

STUDY OF NUDE WITH FIGURE IN MIRROR, 1969

SECOND VERSION OF BULLFIGHT No. 1, 1969

A prodigy at work: Wolfgang Amadeus Mozart, aged eight, performs in a trio with his father and sister.

"...the most gifted human being that has ever been born"

So said Sacheverell Sitwell of—who else?—Wolfgang Amadeus Mozart

"In reality every child is to a certain extent a genius and every genius to a certain extent a child," says Arthur Schopenhauer when he discusses genius in *The World as Will and Idea.* His example, of course, is Mozart. (Whenever we talk about "genius," don't we always begin with Mozart, and are then hard put to find others who can be mentioned in the same breath?) Schopenhauer concluded that a genius, as opposed to a mere man of talent, has to look at the world through childlike eyes as something alien and strange, like a stage play seen from a distance; a genius ought not to be involved in the everyday affairs of this world. Mozart must have been like that, Schopenhauer believed, since it was said of him that "although he had early become a man in his art, yet in all other respects he always remained a child."

Attractive as this theory sounds, one wonders what Mozart would have made of it; he himself never liked to be reminded that the child is the father of the genius. "What annoys me most of all here," he wrote his father from Paris, aged twenty-two, "is that these stupid Frenchmen seem to think I am still seven years old, because that was my age when they first saw me."* And although he was demonstrably inept when it came to paying his bills, financial irresponsibility is not enough to qualify him as a wide-eyed innocent. On the whole, he was neither more nor less practical than the other impoverished musicians of his time. For the most part, he managed to muddle through quite creditably, drawing on ample reserves of mother wit and plain common sense. Toward the end of his life, certainly, Mozart was more man than most, and far more mature as an artist: only a man who has come to grips with the real world could have written a work like *Don Giovanni*, with the richness of experience and insight that are reflected on every page.

Consider *Don Giovanni* for a moment—not only as a perfect example of Mozart's achievement but as a source of continuing joy and wonderment to the best brains of Western civilization. The opera was written in 1787. Can you think of anything else written at that time—not Goethe's iambic *Iphigenie,* surely, or Gibbon's *Decline and Fall,* or even the United

*Mozart's letters to his family are taken from the translation by Emily Anderson.

States Constitution—that still has remotely the same power to fascinate our minds while arousing our passions? For the past two centuries *Don Giovanni* has been like a beacon that always illuminates some new aspect of the intellectual landscape. It has served musicians as a constant point of reference—and it has provided the literati with endless grist for their mill.

For the novelist E. T. A. Hoffmann this music marked the beginning of the romantic movement. To the psychoanalyst Otto Rank it was a great Oedipal drama. In his extraordinary essay *Die Don-Juan Gestalt* (Leipzig, 1924) Rank depicts the Stone Guest as the vengeful spirit of the murdered Ur-father; Leporello as the inseparable voice of his master's conscience; and the Don himself as the liberated Oedipus who has no qualms about killing the primal Ur-father in order to satisfy his lust for the Ur-mother: "The overwhelming greatness of the Don Juan *Gestalt* lies in the fact that he has shed the heroic lie . . ."

This is a far cry from what Karl Barth, the great Swiss Protestant theologian, heard in Mozart's music. Were he a Catholic, Barth said, he would propose Mozart for sainthood, because he was so obviously in touch with the angels. André Gide, on the other hand, used the same music to bolster his own atheist position. Mozart's *tranquillité satisfaite, souriante et reposée,* he said, places him among the great pagan, anti-Christian spirits, in opposition to the (Christian) "anguish and discontent of a Michelangelo, a Beethoven or a Dante." But it is Sören Kierkegaard who saw Mozart's *Don Giovanni* as the ecstatic principle of life itself:

This power in Don Giovanni, this omnipotence, this vitality, can be expressed only in music, and I know no other term for it than this: it is life-expanding joy. . . . Hear him at the beginning of his life, flashing out of the dark thunderclouds like a bolt of lightning . . . hear him as he casts himself into the manifold turmoil of life . . . hear these light, dancing violin notes, hear the beckoning of pleasure, hear the shouts of joy, the festive happiness of contentment; hear his wild chase, how he overtakes himself, always faster, and more indomitable; hear the uncontrollable desire of passion, the roar of love, the whisper of temptation, the whirl of seduction, hear the stillness of the moment—hear, hear, oh hear Mozart's *Don Giovanni!*

"I am in love with Mozart like a young girl," Kierkegaard confessed in *Either/Or:* "Immortal Mozart! I owe you everything; it is thanks to you that I lost my reason, that my soul was awestruck in the very depths of my being. . . . Thanks to you I did not go through life without having encountered something that could shatter me. I have you to thank for the fact that I did not die without having loved . . ."

What sort of man can provoke such impassioned outbursts, though the very word "Mozartean" is supposed to mean smooth, graceful, elegant? A pure spirit "but not pure out of ignorance," as Busoni says; a man with his head in the clouds but fast and light on his feet; a dutiful son who regularly defied his parents; a composer of great tragicomedies because his own character was tragicomic.

His life is often like something out of

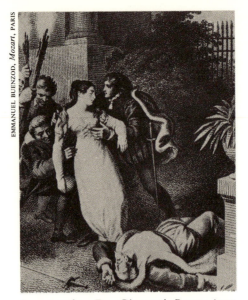

In a scene from Don Giovanni, *Donna Anna swoons at the sight of her murdered father.*

the Theatre of the Absurd: little Mozart, knee-high to a viola da gamba and wearing court dress (hand-me-down clothes that had belonged to the parsimonious royal family of Austria), playing the harpsichord before the crowned ears of Europe; adolescent Mozart in Rome, decorated by the pope with the highest class of the Order of the Golden Spur, but afterward unable to make use of his knighthood because the genuine aristocrats wouldn't tolerate a title acquired by a fluke; twenty-two-year-old Mozart adrift in Paris, a young man with a brilliant future behind him. And then, Mozart in his thirties, in the fullness of his genius, desperately eager to compose but unable to find a patron, though the cognoscenti were well aware that he was the foremost composer of his day. As old Haydn told Mozart's father in 1785, after an evening of chamber music at which they had tried out some new Mozart quartets: "I tell you before God and as an honest man, that your son is the greatest composer I know, either personally or by name. He has taste, and apart from that the greatest science in composition."

That unsolicited testimonial must have come as balm to the anxieties of the elder Mozart, a man full of wise counsels and dire prophecies (usually correct but unheeded) about the consequences of his son's mistakes. Leopold was very much the dominant fig-

ure in his son's life; even when he was no longer on hand to guide Wolfgang's career, he still loomed sternly in the background, like the admonitory statue of the Stone Guest. Mozart the *Wunderkind* was to a large extent his father's invention, for it was Leopold who supplied not only the whole of his musical education but also the genes that prodigies presumably require, along with the energy and ambition to translate the result into something like show business. Mozart's mother, née Anna Maria Pertl, was so self-effacing and anonymous as hardly to have entered into the equation. In Pitts Sanborn's memorably orotund phrase, Mozart "owed all to the unfathomable and inscrutable largesse of Mother Nature in collaboration with the intelligent and inexorable training imposed by an earthly father."

Inexorable is a good description of Leopold, who was a German father of the old school—earnest, dedicated, God-fearing, and conscientious. A self-made man, he came from an obscure family in Augsburg but attended the University of Salzburg before entering the service of the prince-archbishops of Salzburg. He was the author of an important book on violin playing and ultimately became first violinist and Vice-Kapellmeister of the archiepiscopal court. He and his wife, the daughter of a local civil servant, were said to have been the handsomest couple in town, but of their seven children only two survived: Nannerl, a clavier prodigy in her own right, born in 1751, and Wolfgang Amadeus, born on January 27, 1756.

Since the Mozart household in the center of Salzburg constantly reverberated with music, the boy was brought up steeped in sound, and began to make recognizable music of his own at the age of four. He had perfect pitch—i.e., the ability to identify any note without a reference tone—and such a phenomenal sonic memory that he could make mental comparisons between remembered pitches. "Herr Schachtner," he once told a visiting musician, "your violin is half a quarter of a tone lower than mine, that is, if it is tuned as it was when I played on it last."

"I laughed at this," Schachtner later wrote to Wolfgang's sister, "but your father, who knew the wonderful ear and memory of the child, begged me to fetch the violin, and see if he was right. I did, and right he was, sure enough!"

Schachtner, whose reminiscences are the chief source of information about Mozart's early childhood, says that "as soon as he began to give himself to music, his mind was as good as dead to all other concerns, and even his childish games and toys had to be accompanied by music." When someone made him a present of his first violin, he insisted on being allowed to play it in a string trio with his father's friends, though he had never had violin lessons. When Leopold refused, "Wolfgang began to cry bitterly, and slunk away with his little violin. I interceded for him to be allowed to play with me, and at last his father said: 'Play with Herr Schachtner then, but not so as to be heard, or you must go away at once.' So it was settled, and Wolfgang played with me. I soon remarked with astonishment that I was quite superfluous; I put my violin quietly down, and looked at your father, down whose cheeks tears of wonder and delight were running; and so he played all the six trios."

When Wolfgang was six, Leopold decided it was time "to proclaim to the world a prodigy that God has vouchsafed to be born in Salzburg. . . . it becomes my obligation to convince the world of this miracle . . ." He took the two children on the first of a long series of concert tours that were to cover most of western Europe, advertising them as "a girl aged eleven years who plays the most difficult sonatas and concertos . . . on the clavecin or harpsichord with the most distinct execution" and "a boy of six . . . playing the same sonatas, trios, and concertos manfully, not at all like a child . . ."

In Vienna Wolfgang was allowed to jump into the empress Maria Theresa's ample lap; in France he played at Ver-

The merry side of genius came out in Mozart's letters to his cousin Maria Anna.

sailles and was offended when Mme de Pompadour refused his kisses; in England he was warmly received by George III and played fugues with Johann Christian Bach, the youngest of Sebastian's sons. "When Bach . . . had begun a fugue and left off abruptly . . . little Mozart hath immediately taken it up, and worked it after a most masterly manner," reported the British naturalist Daines Barrington in one of his "philosophical transactions." Barrington also provides a detailed account of what it was like when the nine-year-old was asked to improvise a "Song of Rage" for a hypothetical opera:

The boy again looked back with much archness, and began five or six lines of a jargon recitative proper to precede a *Song of Anger.* . . . in the middle of it, he had worked himself up to such a pitch, that he beat his harpsichord like a person possessed, rising sometimes in his chair. The word he pitched upon for this . . . extemporary composition was, *Perfido.* After this he played a difficult lesson, which he had finished a day or two before: his execution was amazing, considering that his little fingers could scarcely reach a fifth on the harpsichord. . . . He was also a great master of modulation, and his transitions from one key to another were excessively natural and judicious; he practiced in this manner for a considerable time with an handkerchief over the keys of the harpsichord.

This extraordinary gift for modu-

lation was always one of the hallmarks of Mozart's style; if he was a "master" of the art at nine, he was a sheer miracle-worker in later years, after he had developed a harmonic subtlety and breadth unequaled by any other composer. His rites of passage as he moves from one key into another are central to the Mozartean conception of music, for it is the modulations that account for the extraordinary poignance of works like the G Minor String Quintet. Harmonically, it is sometimes as though he were taking you into a very plain building to show you only the simplest kinds of décor, and then suddenly throwing open a shuttered window to reveal a magnificent and unsuspected view of the surrounding countryside.

Often he is almost monotonously repetitive in his chords before commencing an elaborate departure into flights of modulation. The A Minor Rondo for piano, for example, begins innocuously enough with a quiet theme accompanied by shadowy chords. But once the basic key has been established, the composition soars off into a series of chromatic arabesques that ravish the ear with the sweet agony of harmonies in constant transition and collision. These tonal deceptions are always very carefully prepared, however; not for Mozart are the sudden shocks and *volte-face* modulations of Joseph Haydn, and still less the "clumsy plunging" with which some of his lesser contemporaries peppered their works.

"He modulates in such a violent way as to make you think that he is resolved to drag you with him by the scruff of the neck," he wrote to his father after hearing the Mannheim composer Joseph Vogler. And again, when he first heard the music of Friedrich Graf in 1777: "He often plunges into a new key far too brusquely and it is all quite devoid of charm." To show how it ought to be done, Mozart proceeded to give a practical demonstration. "Herr Graf, who is Director here, stood there transfixed, like someone who has always imagined that his wanderings from key to key are quite unusual and now finds that one can be even more unusual and yet not offend the ear. In a word, they were all astounded." This was typical of the object lessons he used to give, *en passant*, while cutting a swath through the musical world. And then he wondered why he had so many jealous rivals who tried to make life hard for him.

Of all the stopping places on Mozart's grand tour, it was operatic Italy that gave him the greatest pleasure and recognition. Not only did the pope decorate him; the venerable Accademia Filarmonia of Bologna elected him to membership at fourteen—the youngest musician in its history—after he had demonstrated his ability to write the most difficult sort of counterpoint. Better yet, he won his golden spurs as a composer of Italian operas that found favor even with the hypercritical Milanese. Since he spoke Italian fluently, he felt very much at home there amid the frenetic bustle of cities full of music. In 1772 he wrote cheerfully to his sister Nannerl, who had remained in Salzburg: "Upstairs we have a violinist, downstairs another one, in the next room a singing-master who gives lessons, and in the other room opposite ours an oboist. That is good fun when you are composing! It gives you plenty of ideas."

Would success spoil Amadeus Mozart? Perhaps the real wonder of this *Wunderkind* is that it couldn't, any more than adversity could spoil him later on. Most musical prodigies begin to falter sometime late in adolescence and never regain their original momentum; it seems to take a special sort of tenacity to overcome the disadvantages of a too-spectacular head start in life. Perhaps it was Mozart's well-developed sense of his own worth that carried him past the dead point in the next phase of the cycle, when he was no longer young enough to qualify as a prodigy but was merely a young man with a lot of talent and no particular prospects. "I am a composer

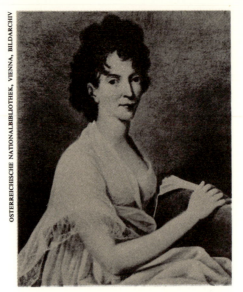

Mozart's "little wife," Constanze, beloved and indulged, appears in an 1802 portrait.

and was born to be a *Kapellmeister*," he wrote Leopold, who had suggested that he might earn a living by teaching, "and I neither can nor ought to bury the talent for composition with which God in his goodness has so richly endowed me (I may say so without conceit, for I feel it now more than ever) . . ."

Hard times in Salzburg were instrumental in helping him come of age—or at least they furnished him, at twenty-two, with a pretext for slipping discreetly away from paternal supervision. A new prince-archbishop, Hieronymus Colloredo, preferred to keep his musicians at home minding the palace, and when Mozart set out on his next tour, Leopold was obliged to remain in Salzburg with Nannerl, while his wife went along to keep an eye on things. Leopold's misgivings about this arrangement were quickly confirmed. Frau Mozart died in Paris after a brief illness, and Wolfgang, left to his own devices, seemed well on his way to becoming an incorrigible spendthrift and a rebel. The change is noted in a letter charged with paternal exasperation. "My Son! You are hot-tempered and impulsive in all your ways! Since your childhood and boyhood your whole character has changed. As a child and a boy you were serious rather than childish and when you sat at the clavier or were otherwise intent on music, no one dared make the slight-

est jest . . . But now, as far as I can see, you are much too ready to retort in a bantering tone to the first challenge—and that, of course, is the first step toward undue familiarity . . ."

But Mozart had a legitimate grievance against a system of patronage that gave the aristocracy a virtual stranglehold on the arts. "I am surrounded by mere brute beasts," he wrote from the heart of fashionable Paris, relating in some detail what a privilege it had been to give a private recital for the Duchesse de Chabot:

I had to wait for half an hour in a large ice-cold, unheated room, which hadn't even a fireplace. At last the Duchesse de Chabot appeared. She was very polite and asked me to make the best of the clavier in the room, as none of her own were in good condition. Would I perhaps try it? I said that I should be delighted to play something, but that it was impossible at the moment, as my fingers were numb with cold; and I asked her to have me taken at least to a room where there was a fire. "*Oh oui, Monsieur, vous avez raison*," was all the reply I got. She then sat down and began to draw and continued to do so for a whole hour, having as company some gentlemen, who all sat in a circle round a big table, while I had the honor to wait. The windows and doors were open and not only my hands but my whole body and my feet were frozen and my head began to ache. There was *altum silentium* and I did not know what to do for cold, headache and boredom. . . . At last, to cut my story short, I played on that miserable, wretched pianoforte. But what vexed me most of all was that Madame and all her gentlemen never interrupted their drawing for a moment, but went on intently, so that I had to play to the chairs, tables and walls. Under these detestable conditions I lost my patience. I therefore began to play the Fischer variations and after playing half of them I stood up. Whereupon I received a shower of *éloges*.

Mozart's real greatness as a composer began precisely at the point where he turned his back on rococo etiquette and struck out into the uncharted regions of a subjective, utterly personal music. Not that he was a willful revolutionary, like Beethoven, deliberately setting out to disturb the peace; Mozart's was a quiet revolution, occurring almost *sotto voce* in the inner voices of his string quartets, in the long, arching andantes of his piano concertos, and in the breathtaking multiplicity of his operatic ensembles, in which half a dozen characters, each expressing his own feelings, unite to form a perfect harmonic nexus that also sums up the dramatic situation of the moment. This is a revolution of sensibility, and it accounts for the curious paradox that Mozart, the embodiment if not the founder of classicism in music, is also the one who sounds the first unmistakably romantic note.

Romanticism in music is a quality quite impossible to define—"Music begins where words fail," Heine says. But whatever it may be, it makes its first appearance in pure, undiluted form in music like the slow movement of the Piano Concerto No. 21, with its gradual unfolding of a theme that takes a leisurely stroll down a chromatic staircase while the chords change, vibrantly, beneath it. This is the gentle side of Mozart's romanticism, the one that Stendhal evokes in his private diaries:

In the moments of dreamy and enchanting melancholy that you find at the end of autumn in the vicinity of an ancient castle under the long pathways of sycamores where the all-embracing silence is disturbed from time to time only by the rustle of the falling leaves, it is the genius of Mozart you love to come across. You wish to hear one of his airs played in the forest by a distant horn.

There is also that darker, more visceral side to Mozart that E. T. A. Hoffmann heard in the overture to *Don Giovanni,* with its "terrifying anticipations of the Unspeakable" and its tremendous conflict "between the nature of man and the cruel, unknown powers that lure him to destruction." What is so fascinating about Mozart's later works, especially *Don Giovanni,* is that the Speakable and the Unspeakable manage to get along so well together; that melancholy and laughter and life

This 1789 sketch of Mozart proved to be the last; he died in 1791 at the age of thirty-five.

and death can coexist in musical time-space. This chiaroscuro mixture, with its beautifully ambiguous effects (is *Don Giovanni* an opera buffa or an *opera seria?* The libretto evades the issue by calling itself a *dramma giocoso,* a "cheerful drama"), is one of Mozart's unique achievements. The later romantics tried for something similar, but they never discovered the secret of his alloy; it isn't enough merely to have saints and sinners on the same stage.

Mozart himself, of course, is a chiaroscuro personality, with a penchant for self-contradiction. Perhaps it had something to do with the fact that he was a very small man, with a frail physique but the temperament of a Titan. "Mozart never reached his natural growth," reports Heinrich von Schlichtegroll, who wrote his account with Nannerl's assistance. "During his whole life, his health was delicate. He was thin and pale, and though the form of his face was unusual, there was nothing striking in his physiognomy but its extreme variableness. The expression of his countenance changed every moment, but indicated nothing more than the pleasure or pain which he experienced at the instant. . . . His body was perpetually in motion; he was either playing with his hands, or beating the ground with his foot."

The Irish tenor Michael Kelly (billed as "Signor Ochelly" when he sang the

first Basilio in *The Marriage of Figaro* in 1786) adds to this portrait in his *Reminiscences:*

He was a remarkably small man, very thin and pale, with a profusion of fine hair, of which he was rather vain. . . . He was remarkably fond of punch, of which beverage I have seen him take copious draughts. He was also fond of billiards, and had an excellent billiard table in his house. Many and many a game have I played with him, but always came off second best. He gave Sunday concerts, which I always attended. He was kind-hearted, and always ready to oblige, but so very particular when he played that, if the slightest noise were made, he instantly left off.

Mozart's friends were treated to an unending stream of pranks, puns, and practical jokes, which not even the most solemn occasions could discourage. Shortly after the première of *The Magic Flute,* for example, he proudly wrote to his wife:

. . . during Papageno's aria with the *Glockenspiel* I went behind the scenes, as I felt a sort of impulse to-day to play it myself. Well, just for fun, at the point where Schikaneder [who sang Papageno] has a pause, I played an arpeggio. He was startled, looked behind the wings and saw me. When he had his next pause, I played no arpeggio. This time he stopped and refused to go on. I guessed what he was thinking and again played a chord. He then struck the [stage] *Glockenspiel* and said "Shut up." Whereupon everyone laughed. I am inclined to think that this joke taught many of the audience for the first time that Papageno does not play the instrument himself.

These puckish tendencies were not exactly helpful to an office seeker in the protocol-ridden eighteenth century, and Mozart never found the powerful patron who would have smoothed the way for him. He was too brash for Paris, had too little influence in Munich, and had too many rivals in Vienna. For a time, a stopgap solution was found for him in Salzburg, though the archbishop took a rather dim view of the prodigal returned: he was appointed court and cathedral organist at a salary of 400 guldens a year, just below the poverty line. Life in Salzburg, moreover, was far too confining for Mozart's taste. "I detest Salzburg," he wrote to a friend, "—and not only on account of the injustices which my dear father and I have endured there . . . Salzburg is no place for my talent. In the first place, professional musicians there are not held in much consideration; and, secondly, one hears nothing, there is no theatre, no opera; and even if they really wanted one, who is there to sing?"

His patience finally snapped when he was made to sit at the valets' table during one of the archbishop's state visits to Vienna. Their last interview terminated (as Mozart tells it) with the following dialogue:

MOZART: So Your Grace is not satisfied with me?

ARCHBISHOP: What, you dare to threaten me—you scoundrel? There is the door! Look out, for I will have nothing more to do with such a miserable wretch.

MOZART: Nor I with you!

ARCHBISHOP: Well, be off!

From then on, Mozart lived in Vienna as a free lance, giving concerts and piano lessons, accompanying singers, and composing music on commission. He might have fared quite well had he not promptly fallen in love. At twenty-five he suddenly felt a pressing need for matrimony: "The voice of nature speaks as loud in me as in others, louder, perhaps, than in many a big strong lout of a fellow." Besides, as he explained to Leopold, "owing to my disposition, which is more inclined to a peaceful and domesticated existence than to revelry, I who from my youth up have never been accustomed to look after my own belongings, linen, clothes and so forth, cannot think of anything more necessary to me than a wife. . . . I am absolutely convinced that I should manage better with a wife (on the same income which I have now) than I do by myself. And how many useless expenses would be avoided! . . . A bachelor, in my opinion, is only half alive."

Famous last words. The girl of his choice was Constanze Weber, daughter of a musician and younger sister of a soprano with whom Mozart had fallen in love on one of his concert tours. Describing her to his father, he carefully refrains from making her sound too attractive: "She is not ugly, but at the same time far from beautiful. Her whole beauty consists in two little black eyes and a pretty figure." Most biographers depict Constanze as a liability that Mozart could ill afford: frivolous, thoughtless, unaware until years later that she was married to a genius, perhaps something of a flirt and a schemer, and certainly no match for Mozart on any level but the bed. Still, except on the occasions when she gave him cause for jealousy, Mozart was happy with her for the rest of his life. He himself, after all, had no more idea than his giddy wife that he was destined to go down in the pages of history as a Great Man.

He never stopped doting on her. After seven years of marriage he was still in the habit of addressing her in the peculiar mixture of word games and baby talk that was his favorite epistolary style. "Dearest, most beloved little Wife," he wrote while on a concert tour. "If I were to tell you all the things I do with your dear portrait . . . For instance, when I take it out of its case, I say, 'Good-day, Stanzerl!—Good-day, little rascal, pussy-pussy, little turned-up nose, little bagatelle, Schluck und Druck,' and when I put it away again, I let it slip in very slowly, saying all the time 'Nu-Nu-Nu-Nu!' with the peculiar emphasis which this word so full of meaning demands, and then just at the last, quickly, 'Good night, little mouse, sleep well.' "

It was during these years that Lorenzo Da Ponte came to Vienna—a poet disguised as an abbé, a baptized Jew from Venice: accomplished libertine, humorist, humanist, court playwright to the emperor Joseph II, and probably the best opera librettist ever to set pen to paper. For the first and last time in his life, Mozart worked with texts that were worthy of his music: "The best thing of all is when a good composer, who understands the stage and is talented enough to make sound suggestions, meets an able poet, that true phoenix . . ."

The first collaboration between the nightingale and the phoenix produced *The Marriage of Figaro* based on Beaumarchais's subversive play, which had been banned from the imperial stages but was now smuggled into the opera house by the back door—slightly expurgated, yet all the more powerful as a piece of prerevolutionary theatre. *Figaro* made a name for them not only in Vienna but also in Prague, where it scored an instant sensation. "Here they talk about nothing but *Figaro*," Mozart was happy to report. "Nothing is played, sung, or whistled but *Figaro*. No opera is drawing like *Figaro*. Nothing, nothing but *Figaro*. Certainly a great honor for me!"

When he played the piano in Prague for the first time, following a performance of the Prague Symphony, composed especially for the concert, the audience could hardly restrain itself. "Never before had the theatre been so crowded as it was on this occasion," wrote the Czech critic Franz Nemecek. "Never before had there been such overwhelming and unanimous ecstasy as his divine playing aroused. We truly did not know which we ought to admire the more, the extraordinary compositions or the extraordinary playing. Both together produced a total effect upon our souls which resembled a sweet enchantment."

Riding the crest of their enthusiasm, Mozart was commissioned to write a new work for the Prague Opera. Apparently the idea of taking Don Juan as the subject stemmed from Da Ponte. He notes in his *Memoirs* (written years later, when he was living in New York) that he set to work on the libretto in great haste, "a bottle of Tokay wine to my right, an inkwell in the middle, and a box of Sevilla tobacco to my left. A beautiful sixteen-year-old girl whom I should have loved as my daughter only—but—, lived in

A concert in the era of Mozart: ten elegantly poised musicians, four of whom are vocalists, give a recital in Barcelona around 1780. The drawing is a contemporary sketch done by Manuel Tramullas.

the same house with me, with her mother. She took care of the household and had permission to enter my room when I rang (which I very often did)—particularly when my inspiration began to cool off)."

If the story is true—Da Ponte has to be taken with a grain of salt—it would account for the lusty odor of sex and verisimilitude that pervades the seduction scenes of *Don Giovanni.* As for Mozart's inspiration, it never cooled off; he seems to have completed the opera in Vienna between the middle of May and the end of August, 1787, then gone to Prague for the rehearsals. The much-disputed story that he wrote the Overture on the night before the première, while his wife plied him with punch and told jokes to keep him awake, is corroborated by the manuscript, which bears signs of having been written in great haste and at a single sitting. Apparently he had been carrying the music in his head for some time, since he couldn't have composed it at that speed.

He seems to have had no inkling he had created a work that would, like *Hamlet,* remain a source of perpetual fascination to people both inside the theatre and out of it. From the very first chords of the Overture, prophesying that the grave will spew up the ghost of the Stone Guest, the gates swing open on the romantic age, and on an entirely new conception of what could be expressed in art. *Don Giovanni* is so heavily charged with symbolism that it took Otto Rank eighty pages to describe its psychoanalytic significance, but the key to its power is in the indescribable music: "hear, hear, oh hear Mozart's *Don Giovanni!*"

Mozart and Da Ponte created one further masterpiece together, though it has no more significance than a set of Dresden china figurines: *Così fan Tutte* (Women Are All Like That). The German opera that followed, *Die Zauberflöte* (The Magic Flute), has a boring patchwork libretto by Schikaneder that is redeemed by some of Mozart's finest music.

During these final years he was pursued by financial troubles. Though he had obtained a small stipend as nominal "composer to the imperial court," he was forced to appeal to his friends for charity disguised as loans. During that miraculous summer of 1788, for example, while he was composing the last three symphonies—No. 39 in E Flat, No. 40 in G Minor, and No. 41 in C, the Jupiter—he had to write his fellow Freemason Michael Puchberg to say that he was finding it impossible to keep his affairs in order; if he could borrow some money, "then, *primo . . .* I can meet necessary expenses whenever they occur . . . *secondo,* I can work with a mind more free from care and with a lighter heart, and thus earn more."

The symphonies reveal nothing of all this. The passionate discontent one hears in the G Minor Symphony or the G Minor String Quintet belongs to another order of anguish than that reflected in his letters to Puchberg: "I beg you to lend me until to-morrow at least a couple of hundred *gulden,* as my landlord in the Landstrasse has been so importunate that in order to avoid an unpleasant incident I have had to pay him on the spot, and this has made things very awkward for me!"

These troubles could not reach his music, but in the end they destroyed him physically. The trajectory of his life had been moving steadily upward, fulfilling the promise of his early genius; suddenly it took a sharp downturn and then, without warning, was cut short in mid-flight at the age of thirty-five. He was, of course, hard at work when he fell ill—on an unfinished Requiem Mass that had been commissioned by an agent for an "unknown gentleman," whom Mozart instinctively recognized as the messenger of death. Many doctors believe that he died of nephritis, but one modern source says it was rheumatic fever and an ensuing cardiac collapse; we know that he remained conscious to the end and that he died "calmly but most unwillingly."

"On the day of his death," Nemecek records, "he had the score brought to his bed. 'Didn't I prophesy I was writing this Requiem for myself?' So he spoke and looked through the whole thing attentively once more with wet eyes. It was the last anguished look of parting from his beloved art."

Much has been made of the fact that his widow and friends allowed his body to be buried in an unmarked grave. But Mozart did have mourners, including many distinguished citizens, who attended his funeral in St. Stephen's Cathedral in Vienna. It was then customary for ordinary people's coffins to remain in the "Death Chapel" until evening, when they were transported to the cemetery for interment, usually in unmarked graves. That this happened in Mozart's case is merely another indication that he did not belong to the "real" nobility. But the distinction had never troubled him: "It is the heart that ennobles a man; and though I am no count, yet I have probably more honour in me than many a count." Monuments to him, in any case, are not lacking in Vienna and elsewhere; some of them bear a striking resemblance to the Stone Guest. That his spirit still walks abroad, no musician will deny.

The Impossibility of Dropping Out

Fleeing the "system," many now seek individuality in tight-knit "sensitivity" groups.

The counter culture—whatever its
historical precedents,
whatever the worthiness of its aims
—must inevitably discover
that from technocracy there *is* no escape

By ANTHONY HARTLEY

There is an archetypal plot that occurs in much contemporary science fiction, though it dates at least from H. G. Wells's 1899 novel *When the Sleeper Wakes.* Society is ruled by a technocratic oligarchy. Every action of every human being is regulated. Thought control has gone so far that most people do not even wish to revolt; they are willing serfs of the machine. But there is one man who does rebel against the controllers. He is persecuted and pursued, but manages to awaken in others the same spark that is in him. The iron society that weighs on mankind is overthrown . . . or else the Promethean hero dies.

Science fiction is so widely read these days that it is certainly legitimate to find in much of what it has to say the unconscious expression of our time. Moreover, in the theme just described there is so great a coincidence with much young radical thought that the two may reasonably be regarded as coming from the same source—profound dissatisfaction with the bureaucratic mechanism of an advanced industrial society.

Behind the hippie communes, behind the escape from reality provided by drugs, behind the concern for the environment and the movement to get back to nature, can be discerned a distaste for the oppressiveness of a society that imprisons so many people in offices, records their doings in data banks and social security archives, and expects them to go from the cradle to the grave with the virtues of punctuality, sobriety, and application. The "power structure" denounced by radicals is not just a political system. It is felt by them to be a way of life that weighs upon us all.

Rightly or wrongly, these are objections to a certain form of order. And it is interesting to ask ourselves whether, at any period of history, men have felt similarly stifled by an all-pervading order.

In most cases, of course, the reverse has been true. The Anglo-Saxons, thankful for a year of respite from Viking raiders, looked for a strong king to defend them. In Shakespeare's history plays, weakness in a ruler is considered the ultimate disaster, leading to anarchy and civil war. At moments of upheaval such as the French Revolution, tyranny has been more easily supported than anarchy. Human history has been dominated by the desire for an ordered society—often to the detriment of those very individuals who chose a "strong" man or a party of "order" only to find they had created a system of lawful illegality, an order of criminal anarchy.

So it is not easy to find historical precedents for the peculiar malaise that our advanced industrial society causes. Yet there are some suggestive parallels. The monks and hermits who at the beginning of the fourth century went into the deserts of Roman Egypt to fast and pray were certainly motivated by religious feelings, but also by a more human desire to escape from a society in which the hand of landlords and a tax-collecting bureaucracy had become unbearably heavy. One terrible feature of the Roman (and the Chinese) Empire was that there was no real escape from oppression. A civilized Roman could not find among the Goths across the Danube or among the nomads of the Arabian peninsula the cultivated urban society that made life worth living. If he offended the emperor, he could submit to savage punishment, open his veins, or go into the miserable exile of Ovid, who spent his last years remembering Italy beside the Black Sea.

Given these conditions, it is not surprising that the caves and deserts of Egypt seemed to offer the possibility of an "interior emigration" more agreeable than flight to the court of a barbarian chieftain. The ascetics led by Saint Anthony, who sought to avoid the pressures of society, formed the communes of their day, though their visions and ecstasies were attained without hallucinogenic drugs or free love.

It may well be the very universality of our technological civilization that is intimidating. There is no refuge from social security cards, tax forms, university degrees, registration with the police (if you happen to be residing in a foreign country), no recourse from the whole bureaucratic apparatus with which the advanced industrial state governs, more or less benevolently, its citizens. It is probably less easy to lead the life of a hermit today than it was in fourth-century Egypt, and as for living the simple life of a poet, one has only to look at the appalling entanglements with the British Board of Inland Revenue that darkened the end of Dylan Thomas's life to see how vainly the "beautiful and ineffectual angels" of our own day beat their wings against a sky of bronze—or paper.

Much of the contemporary resentment against the power structure is due to a kind of claustrophobia that overcomes the young as they contemplate the evident impossibility of dropping out of a society that will close around them even more tightly when they leave their schools and universities and enter the world of offices and commuter trains. The joys of the Polynesian long house that now accompany adolescence in Western industrial countries make this prospect all the more somber. Nothing, obviously, will ever be as nice again, or as good, as it was when they were seventeen.

Like the elite of the Roman Empire, the young today perceive with resignation or despair that most of their pleasures are intimately connected with a form of society they feel to be oppressive. Who will produce for them the cars, the hi-fi equipment, the electric guitars, that form an essential part of the youth culture, if not the corporations against which they direct their rebellion? The spectacle of communes devoted to simple living and the cult of nature, but surrounded by piles of tin cans, bears melancholy witness to this paradox. The youth culture is against pollution, but it is the internal-combustion engine that has given the young

the freedom from the family that is essential to their existence. There is no absolute escape, nor is it certain that these refugees from the power structure would wish one.

Theodore Roszak's "counter culture" or Charles Reich's "Consciousness III" can be seen as attempts to establish a theoretical basis for the internal emigration of the young, to produce a City of God alongside the secular, industrial state. But, unlike Saint Augustine's massive construction of a countersociety, theirs have about them all the impermanence of the young for whom they are intended. Perhaps internal emigration is only possible when it applies to a representative section of society, not selected by age and not subject to re-entry into the system with the passing of youth. Some religious or philosophical imperative stronger than that gained from a reading of Tolkien or Kahlil Gibran's *The Prophet* is also required.

In fact, advanced industrial society proves itself to be more pervasive even than the bureaucracy of the later Roman Empire. No revolt can help much. Modern man, it seems, will have to live with his claustrophobia, and the unpleasantness of this conclusion for the devotees of Consciousness III will not be mitigated by the fact that the contemporary power structure looks positively benign when compared to old-fashioned tyrannies.

Brook Farm, the Egyptian monks of the Thebaid, the communes of the young—these are no solution in an age when technology and instant communication are forcing upon each of us an increased social responsibility. That such responsibility can seem crushing is undoubted. That it has to be assumed is a condition of life in the twentieth century. The followers of Saint Anthony, after all, eventually emerged from their deserts to change and humanize society.

Anthony Hartley, alien registration number A-17 534 003, wrote Gaullism: the Rise and Fall of a Political Movement.

Bess and Old Noll

Can it be true that

Oliver Cromwell, the sternest Puritan of them all, had a mistress,

a beautiful *Royalist* mistress,

as the old rumor said? The dreadful possibility is herein weighed

By ANTONIA FRASER

She is Bess of my heart, she was Bess of
   Old Noll,
She was once Fleetwood's Bess, now she's
   Bess of Atholl. . . .

So ran a merry jingle in the reign of
Charles II on the subject of the supposed lovers of the powerful—and evidently desirable—Elizabeth, Duchess
of Lauderdale. The rhyme continued in
lines more explicit on the source of the
Duchess's power, and that of her husband—who was virtual dictator of
Scotland for twenty years after the
Restoration:

She's Bess of the Church, and Bess of the
   State
She plots with her tail, and her lord with
   his pate . . .

The beautiful Elizabeth Murray, as
she was born, had married Sir Lionel
Tollemache in 1647, then had become
Countess of Dysart in her own right.
In 1672 she became the second wife of
John Maitland, already Earl and about
to be made Duke of Lauderdale. With
her husband she cut a considerable
dash at the court of Charles II, leaving
quite aside her undoubted display at
the Scottish court, of which Lauderdale was High Commissioner. So regal
was Elizabeth's behavior that she was
acccused of behaving "grander than
the Queen," and there were angry cries
in Scotland that they now had "two
Commissioners."

In England Elizabeth and Lauderdale
held a miniature court of their own at
Ham House on the Thames, Elizabeth's
inheritance, which they renovated with
taste and munificence and which John
Evelyn described lyrically in 1678 as
"inferior to few of the best villas in
Italy itself; the house furnished like a
great prince's; the parterres, flower
gardens, orangeries, groves, avenues,
courts, statues, perspectives, fountains,
aviaries, and all this at the banks of the
sweetest river in the world."

Elizabeth was now a woman of forty-
odd—how odd was a matter of some
dispute, since some of her friends said
she was forty-five when she married

Lauderdale (which would mean she
had been born in 1627), and others
were more uncharitable. It was generally agreed that she was beyond child-
bearing age, but otherwise, her birth
date has always been a mystery, as,
perhaps, befits the nativity of an established beauty.

In the high-living years following
the restoration of the Stuart monarchy,
scurrilous verse was not the only source
for the rumor that the red-haired Duchess was once mistress to Oliver Cromwell—"Old Noll" the Cavaliers had
called him. As a great lady of the court,
with a splendid house at her disposal,
Elizabeth was often visited, admired,
and described by contemporary mem-
oirists. Sir John Reresby, writing in
1677, referred to the famous "fine house
at Ham," and continued in language
more elegant than the verse lampoon
but of similar import: "After dinner
her Grace entertained me in her chamber with much discourse upon affairs
of state. She had been a beautiful woman; the supposed mistress of Oliver
Cromwell; and at that time a lady of
great parts."

For proof of this rela-
tionship, the story most commonly advanced was that Elizabeth had interceded with Cromwell in 1651 to save
the life of Lauderdale. He had been
captured by the Roundheads after the
Battle of Worcester, in which the English and Scottish Royalists had at last
been routed. While his fellow prisoner
the Earl of Derby was executed, Lauderdale was spared, to languish in various
prisons until the Restoration freed him.
Elizabeth at this point was still married to her first husband, and Lauderdale to his first wife, Lady Anne Home;
but at twenty years' distance, what
could be more romantic than the idea
that the future Duchess had pleaded
with one powerful lover, Oliver Cromwell, in order to save the life of another?

To give further plausibility to the

idea of the *affaire*, there was even a
suggestion that Elizabeth's second son,
Thomas Tollemache, born in 1651,
might owe his genesis to the Lord Protector. The coarsest allusion to the
Restoration Duchess consisted of an
imaginary dialogue between Elizabeth's
two husbands, in which Sir Lionel
lamented:

. . . while unmarried, what intrigues she
   kept;
Then, when my wife, what part 'mongst
   whores she bore;

to which the Duke of Lauderdale re-
plied, adding a list of names:

And while your wife, alas! there I did take
As mine what others did behind your back.
The traitor Cromwell, Ross and Broadal-
   bane,
Can tell as well as Atholl and Strathallane . . .

Leaving aside this "list" of Elizabeth's lovers, let us consider Cromwell alone, and the question of whether
there could be any truth in the notion
of a love affair between Bess and Old
Noll. Gilbert Burnet, later Bishop of
Salisbury, had some firsthand knowledge of her history, for Gilbert's wife,
Lady Margaret Kennedy, had once
been courted by Lauderdale and had
heard his own story concerning the
sparing of his life in 1651.

Burnet's account, written around
the turn of the century, gives a lively
character sketch of Elizabeth: "a woman of great beauty, but of far greater
parts," extremely quick in mind and
conversation; one who had studied
mathematics, divinity, history, and
philosophy, but despite, or perhaps
because of, this intellectual training,
"was violent in everything she set about,
a violent friend, but a much more violent enemy." According to Burnet, this
bluestocking termagant "had been early
in a correspondence with Lord Lauderdale, that had given occasion to censure. When he was prisoner after the
Worcester fight, she made him believe
he was in great danger of his life, and
that she saved it by her intrigues with
Cromwell: which was not a little taken

107

notice of. Cromwell was certainly fond of her, and she took care to entertain him in it; till he, finding what was said upon it, broke it off." After the Restoration, Burnet continues, Lauderdale did not reward Elizabeth with the gratitude she had expected, and their relationship was not resumed until after the death of her first husband in 1669.

A similar version of this story is told by Sir George Mackenzie of Rosehaugh, Lord Advocate of Scotland under Charles II and James II. Mackenzie hints at a "fondness" between Cromwell and Elizabeth that masked something deeper, and was certainly strong enough to enable Elizabeth to plead successfully for the life of a traitor in the Tower. Twenty years later, grateful memory of the incident led to love and finally marriage between the prisoner and his fair intercessor. In the meantime, though the decapitated head of the Lord Protector still withered on a spike outside Westminster Hall as a warning to potential usurpers (it was there as late as 1684), the head of his alleged mistress was only enhanced by the sinister halo of her former connection.

*B*ut what was the real truth of the relationship between the aging Lord Protector and the spritely young Elizabeth? Are these Restoration rumors enough to convict Oliver of having been susceptible to at least one extra-marital involvement? Some would find this piece of dalliance a delightful aspect of an otherwise iron character. In order to find out, one must go away from the *louche* atmosphere of the 1670's, far back to the 1640's, when Elizabeth Murray first appeared on the stage of society.

Born into a Scottish family closely connected with Charles I, she was the eldest daughter of William Murray, a confidant of the king since youth, when he had acted as his whipping boy. The early role of scapegoat led to the later role of emissary, and often intriguer, on the king's behalf, and as a reward, in 1643 William Murray was created Earl of Dysart. The earliest description of Elizabeth is that given by Thomas Knyvett, who met her when she was about seventeen. She made a most agreeable impression upon him, and his only criticism was focused on the color of her hair: "[The] eldest daughter is the jewel, and indeed a pretty one but for her deep-coloured hair." Knyvett continued, however: "such a pretty, witty lass, with such a brave house and state as she is like to have, m'thinks might make a young fellow think her hair very beautiful." And, more tolerantly still: "I could find it in my heart to woo her for my son." In short, Elizabeth appeared to be "a very good harmless virtuous witty little babe."

This "virtuous witty little babe" was soon married to Sir Lionel Tollemache, a Suffolk baronet of good family. The youthful portrait of Elizabeth by Lely, still hanging at Ham House, belies Knyvett's criticism of her hair, which Lely shows as sandy-gold, the color of sunshine rather than sunset, and Elizabeth seems also to have enjoyed the delicate pink-and-white complexion of some Scottish redheads. Her nose is long but finely made; her mouth, curling and pink, is neat rather than large; her hands are pleasantly dimpled. Her eyelids, on the other hand, above eyes that are large and almost bulging, are heavy, and already there are faint circles under her eyes (like a child who has stayed up too late). But the whole effect is one of innocence and softness: if sensuality has a place, it is unconscious sensuality.

Indeed, to see how different the young Elizabeth was from the Restoration Duchess, one has only to inspect the later double portrait, also by Lely, of Elizabeth and her second husband. Lauderdale's Duchess is as heavy-set as Lauderdale himself; the sunshine hair has darkened; the circles have become bags. The two portraits illustrate a lady's progress through life, from gaiety to debauchery, as clearly as any series by Hogarth.

No one knows when the young Lady Tollemache first met Oliver Cromwell. Elizabeth's married existence was certainly spent among a circle of friends and relations who were strong Royalists. The Tollemaches lived partly in Suffolk, partly in London, and partly, after 1651, at Ham House. Elizabeth's father had received it as a grant with his peerage, but after the Civil War the property was sequestrated, and not returned until 1651.

Elizabeth provided Sir Lionel with a large family. She bore her first child, a son, in January, 1649, and her second, Thomas, sometime in 1651. In all, she had eleven children, of whom five survived. As a nineteenth-century commentator observed, it was to Elizabeth's credit that in the reign of Charles II "a mother of eleven children can hold her own among the beauties of a court."

But to return to the earlier period of the Commonwealth, when could Elizabeth have possibly achieved enough influence over its rising star to enable her to save Lauderdale's life immediately after Worcester? Oliver Cromwell was unarguably absent from England much of the time in those days. In the critical early months of 1649—the period just after the king's death, when the newborn republic struggled for breath—there are no contemporary references to any love affair of Oliver's, though Royalist abuse along other lines showered plentifully on his martial head. In August, 1649, Cromwell departed for Ireland and did not return until May 29, 1650. He stayed in England for a month, but it is hardly likely that he spent this, the busiest time of his life, besieging a lady. On June 28 he set off on his Scottish campaign, remaining out of the country until September, 1651, when he pursued the Scots south and annihilated them at Worcester. Cromwell and Elizabeth might well have been acquainted or even on friendly terms during this period of tumultuous activity, but any kind of romance must surely belong to the period after Oliver's return from Scotland, the seven years of the Commonwealth and the Protectorate, when he was acknowledgedly the leading man in England.

Elizabeth now queened it at Ham House, while Oliver, Lord Protector after 1653, spent much of his time at nearby Hampton Court, these two red edifices being linked by the river as well as by road. Elizabeth flourished in a London at peace, even if it was a republican peace; the warm breath of pleasure crept back into the atmosphere much more quickly than is sometimes supposed. As John Evelyn reported in May, 1654, the women of London were painting their faces like prostitutes.

Dorothy Osborne, later Lady Temple, gives a vivid portrait of Elizabeth in a letter of about the same date referring to Lady Tollemache as one that "says she can do whatsoever she will," and repeating Elizabeth's own explanation of how she avoided catching smallpox after her physician had told her the spots were already coming out: "but she bethought herself that it was not at all convenient for her to have them at that time," as it happened that she was planning to go abroad. Lady Tollemache announced that she had thus successfully repelled the onslaught of the disease by sheer will power and had never in fact fallen victim to the pox. "Twenty such stories as these she tells; and then falls into discourses of the strength of reason and the power of philosophy, till she confounds herself and all that hear her."

The picture is of a woman beautiful and witty, intelligent, able to take part in good conversation, of a more subtle appeal to a man of Cromwell's serious caliber than a mere siren. In 1651, when he returned after the "crowning mercy"—Worcester, his last battle— Cromwell was fifty-two, which might be considered as at least sixty by the standards of our day. The seven remaining years of his life, although years of increasing power and pomp, were without the certainty of military campaigns. There was no fine undeniable showing of the will of God, no splendid "signs" in the shape of glorious victories, in the complicated and ultimately saddening politics of the Commonwealth and the Protectorate. Oliver looked for God's will in vain in the repeated disillusionments produced by his parliaments. But there were some private joys to atone for the public cares.

As a conscientious parent in the Puritan mold, Oliver took seriously the problems of his sons, Richard and Henry, and of his dutiful daughter Bridget, married first to Cromwell's colleague, Ireton, and then, after his premature death, to another general, Fleetwood. But the two youngest daughters, Mary and Frances, his "little wenches," as he liked to call them, had more carefree spirits. They seemed almost like a second family, being eight and nine years younger than Cromwell's favorite daughter, Elizabeth, or "Bettie."

Mary and Frances behaved as much like royal princesses under their father's Protectorate as they possibly could. Grand matches were considered for them, as if they were members of a real royal family, and even the name of the young bachelor in exile in France, Charles II, was mentioned. Mary, who finally married Viscount Fauconberg, of a Royalist family, and Frances, who married the grandson of the Earl of Warwick, loved to dance and amuse themselves with masks. Like an old bear, Oliver seems to have regarded these frolics on the part of his cubs with indulgence. At the two masks for Mary's wedding to Fauconberg, written for the occasion by Andrew Marvell, Cromwell is even supposed to have acted the nonsinging role of the genial father of the bride.

Though the antics of these uninhibited girls delighted Oliver, his devotion was reserved for his beloved Bettie, wife of John Claypole. Elizabeth Tollemache was about the same age as Bettie Cromwell, and though Oliver the stern Puritan might not have appreciated Elizabeth's company, Oliver the fond father could have done so. One of Oliver's most sympathetic qualities was his need for friendship. As he complained in 1652: "Have I one friend in our society to whom I can unbowell myself? . . . I am left alone—almost so—but not forsaken. Lend me one shoulder. Pray for me." Cromwell also had a curiously modern desire to talk and talk again with those of differing opinions, and he seems to have been susceptible to good company for its own sake.

It must have been Elizabeth's company, and her conversation, that attracted Oliver, already predisposed by the example of his daughters to find the companionship of young women relaxing and agreeable. Bishop Burnet, in referring to the famous "fondness" of Cromwell for Elizabeth, admitted that Oliver ended the relationship as soon as he realized that it was causing gossip. The gossip might well have had some political overtones. Elizabeth was a keen Royalist who, in the later years of the Protectorate, as her correspondence shows, joined in subversive activities against Cromwell. Under the circumstances, her charm might not have weighed as heavily with Oliver as her chicanery. His self-denial of her company may well have been dictated as much by distaste for her conspiratorial involvements as by fear of malicious comment.

Interestingly enough, the most vicious attack on Oliver's character, Heath's *Flagellum,* which is the source book for many of the canards subsequently spread about him, makes no reference to Elizabeth. The best that Heath could do to provide Oliver with a taste for debauchery was to blackguard his reputation with regard to Frances Lambert, the wife of one of his own generals. It seems strange that Heath, writing in 1663, only a few years after Oliver's death, should have ignored the subject of the liaison with Elizabeth if it had really been common knowledge during the Protectorate. If Oliver is to be saddled with a mistress, Frances Lambert would be a more likely candidate than Elizabeth Tollemache. Elizabeth was a Royalist, but Frances belonged to the inner circle of Roundheads. The Reverend Mark Noble's *Memoirs of the Protectorate* (1784) repeats the contemporary witticism that "the protector's instrument (of government) was found under my lady Lambert's petticoat," and relates that Oliver discontinued his visits to "the gay lady Dysart" for fear of the disapproval of the ungodly, "but there could no hurt arise in holding heavenly meditations with Mrs. Lambert."

Frances, too, was charming—"beautiful and showy" Carlyle called her—but her charm and beauty and show were of a different order from that of Elizabeth. Heath's *Flagellum* also recounts the Lambert rumor: "The Voice of the people was, that she was more familiar with him than the honour of her sex would allow, and that she had extraordinary kindnesses for him which she had not for her husband." Yet there is no proof of this, and a study of Cromwell's life and letters, and his known attitude toward his wife, makes it inconceivable that he should have indulged in such a physical amour with either Frances or Elizabeth. Royalists might deride the Lady Protectress for the stinginess of her housekeeping, but she performed most adequately as a political wife, giving her husband the domestic peace that freed his mind to get on with his own concerns. Serenity was the keynote of Oliver's long married life, which began in 1620 and ended with his death. The Lady Protectress may not have been exciting to the outside world, or glamourous, but Oliver, who benefited from her serenity and was indifferent to matters of outward style, was well pleased with her. After they had been married for thirty-one years, he was still able to write his wife tenderly from Scotland that he missed the pleasure of her company.

In personal terms Oliver seems to have led the very model of a happy married life, as laid down in Puritan handbooks of the time. His attitude toward sex was probably well represented by a wise saying in Daniel Rogers's *Matrimoniall Honour* of 1642. "The benefit of the Bed," as it is described in this handbook of the Puritan ideal, results in "fitnesse of body and mind thereby purchased, freely to walk with God and to discharge duties of calling without distraction or annoyance."

ow then should one rate the Restoration gossip about Bess and Old Noll, and Elizabeth's claim that she saved Lauderdale's life after Worcester? For these seem to be the only puzzles that remain after the story of the *affaire* is abandoned. The rumor about Thomas Tollemache's dubious parentage is of a much later date; he was almost certainly conceived while Cromwell was in Scotland and Elizabeth in England.

As to the saving of Lauderdale, there was certainly no reason why Oliver's friendship with Elizabeth should not have led him to perform some specific act of mercy. Oliver was noted for such private acts, particularly toward women. He treated Lady Ormonde kindly, for example, though her husband had led the Royalist armies in Ireland, and "on consideration of her condition," he allowed Anne, Countess of Lauderdale, an income while her husband was in prison.

Nevertheless, saving Lauderdale's life on the petition of a young woman would come into quite a different category. Yet there is no proof—except gossip—that this was why the Scottish lord was spared. Lauderdale, exhausted by the defeat of Worcester and satisfied that the king had escaped, surrendered with others of the Scottish leaders shortly after the battle and was taken to London. Though it was the intention of Parliament to execute the villains of the Scottish revolt—Hamilton, Derby, Cleveland, and the mayor and sheriff of Worcester, along with Lauderdale—the English Earl of Derby perished rather than the Scottish Earl of Lauderdale. There were good reasons for this. After the victory, wrath fell harder on the Englishman who had betrayed his country by joining the Scots than on the Scots themselves. Oliver was no believer in pointless executions. In the aftermath of Worcester, he had problems enough in the young Commonwealth without indulging in a bloodbath.

On his release in 1651 Lauderdale showed no immediate signs of continuing—or initiating—any sort of relationship with Elizabeth. The death of Sir Lionel in Paris in 1669 gave the impetus to their love affair; although Sir Lionel lived abroad a great deal, for reasons of health, he raised no complaints against his wife in England more serious than the fact that her letters were "infrequent." His last will shows that he remained on the fondest of terms with her, and in a Polonius-like letter of advice to his eldest son, written shortly before his death, he specifically begs him not to choose a wife without Elizabeth's consent.

The only hint of Sir Lionel's hidden feelings on the remarkable character of his wife occurs in the same letter, and that indirectly: Sir Lionel advised his son to "love her entirely" but on no account to let her know it, "for all wives are but too apt to take advantage of the fondness of their husband, and upon it to grow insolent and imperious . . . and if she get the reins in her own hands, away she will run with it, you scarce ever will stop her in the whole course of her life." Although Sir Lionel was too discreet to say so, we may guess from this piece of philosophy that it was Elizabeth's strong will—the same will Dorothy Osborne commented on—that caused the storms in their married life, rather than any adulteries she might have committed.

By 1670 Anne, Countess of Lauderdale, had departed to live in Paris, no doubt because of the flagrant love affair between her husband and the widowed Lady Tollemache—a liaison public enough to shock even Charles II's court. Anne Lauderdale thus deserted her London salon, to which Pepys had paid a visit in 1666. The fact that this Scottish hostess south of the Border still patriotically had native airs served up on the "viallin" after dinner may perhaps have contributed something to the alienation of her husband. Pepys reported the said airs dutifully as "the best of their country" before giving his own reaction: "but Lord! the strangest ayre that ever I heard in my life, and all of one cast." Lauderdale then frankly declared to him that he would rather hear a cat mew than the best music in the world, showing the full spectrum of his musical dislike by rating the lute first in order of hatred and then the bagpipes. Even if Anne's Scottish airs were bad enough to escape his severest displeasure—"the better the musique, the more sicke it makes him!"—this vignette given us by Pepys is scarcely indicative of a happy accommodation of different temperaments within one marriage.

*W*hat more likely explanation could there be of the story of the intercession than that Elizabeth herself, to win Lauderdale's interest, told him he owed his life to her—a story hard to disprove after such a long time, since he had manifestly been spared at the last minute, whatever the reason. In July, 1670, eighteen months before their marriage, when Elizabeth was a widow but Lauderdale still wedded to Anne, he wrote a codicil to his will leaving Elizabeth fifteen hundred pounds: "And this as a token of my gratitude for the pains and charges she was at in preserving my life when I was a prisoner in the year 1651 . . ." There is no particular reason why Elizabeth should not have believed the story, if she had

indeed made approaches on Lauderdale's behalf. Thus the legend grew. One may still distinguish between the fact that Elizabeth besought Oliver to save Lauderdale's life and the reason that his life was actually spared. Elizabeth may have been in the position of the legendary rainmaker, who offered to pray for rain and demanded payment by results. She got her results, and her payment—deferred by twenty years—was to marry the most important man in Scotland.

As Duchess of Lauderdale, a splendid haughty figure, Elizabeth was in a position to regale her audience with tales, or at least hints, of her relationship with Cromwell, with no ghosts there to contradict her and much popular interest in the character of the dead usurper. Nowadays the alleged mistress of a former dictator might enjoy much the same prestige. Undoubtedly, Elizabeth's charms were waning with age: the strong will of her youth turned into imperiousness; and the maternal woman turned into a harridan who nearly ruined her brother-in-law with law suits, and argued viciously over the ownership of three swans on a lake. The intelligence, education, and wit that had distinguished her from her contemporaries were used in later years to deprive others of properties rightfully theirs.

A frank exposition of Elizabeth's feelings for Oliver Cromwell exists in a letter (taken from the Tollemache MSS) that she wrote in May, 1659, six months after his death. Elizabeth had, in fact, been in Paris at the time, indulging in a complex if ineffectual Royalist plot. She returned to England at the news of the Protector's death, which she apparently did not regret; she seemed to regard it as a hopeful omen of the eventual return of the king, for which she was working: "It is certain that there is now a great change, but not unexpected to me; on the contrary I ever did believe things would end where they begin. . . ." As for Oliver, "There are in this assembly divers that I know to be very considerable and

some to whom I am obliged, but certainly had *the old one* lived there was none that could say so much or expect the least of reality. I can only say I did know him, and I hope I shall never know his fellow."

At this point, unaware of the rich destiny still ahead of her, Elizabeth moralized on her desire to lead a country life: "my retirement has been of greater use to me than my being in the world, since I am come by the one to discern what the world is to me, and by the other I only knew what it was in itself."

This view of Oliver—a man whose fellow she hopes never to know again—expressed by Elizabeth before the Restoration and in an atmosphere of cool self-examination, is worth more than all the becks and nods and wreathed smiles of her later years. The story of Bess and Old Noll is an example of that type of friendship traditionally considered so rare—friendship between a man and a woman unalloyed by a physical relationship. Let Oliver keep his reputation free at least from the accusation of adultery, since he has charges to contend with at the bar of history for which his admirers need heavier briefs to defend him; and let Elizabeth herself, the aging, litigious, amoral duchess of the reign of Charles, be remembered as she was in her twenties—still not utterly removed from the witty, virtuous babe of Knyvett's ecstatic description. She was then charming, high-spirited, and taking enough to make her company delightful to the old Protector. Inevitably, their paths diverged, but for political rather than emotional reasons—politics, at the time, it seems, being more important than emotions.

Antonia Fraser is well known as the author of Mary Queen of Scots, *the scholarly biography that became a best seller, footnotes and all. She is the daughter of another distinguished biographer, Elizabeth Longford. Lady Antonia is now writing a life of Cromwell, from which this article has been adapted.*

An Encounter

he Year: 452. The Place: the southern
bank of the River Po. The Forelook: curtains
on further hopes of a Western and Christian
    civilization.

For Attila and his Hun horde, slant-eyed, sallow,
the creatures of an animist horse-culture,
dieted on raw meat and goat cheese, nocent to
    cities and letters,

were tented there, having routed the imperial
armies and preyed the luscious north, which now lay
frauded of mobile goods, old sedentary
    structures distorted.

Rome was ghastly. What earthly reason was there
why she should now not be theirs for the taking?
The pope alone kept his cool, to the enemy
    now came in person,

sequenced by psalm-singing monks: astonished,
Attila stared at a manner of men so
unlike his. "Your name?" he snapped at their leader.
    "Leo," he answered, raising

his right hand, the forefinger pointed upward,
the little finger pressed to the thumb, in the
Roman salute: "I ask the king to receive me
    in private audience."

Their parley was held out of earshot; we only
know that it was brief, that suddenly Attila
wheeled his horse and galloped back to the encampment,
    yelling out orders.

Next morning the site was vacant: they had vanished,
never to vex us again. What can Leo have
possibly said? He never told, and the poets
    can only imagine

speeches for those who breathe a common cosmos:
all we can say is that he rose to the occasion,
that for once, and by his own standards, the prince of
    this world showed weakness.

By W. H. AUDEN